THE LAW OF GOD

AND THE

PROPHETS OF ISLAM

BY VAUGHN MARTIN

Vaughn Martin

ISBN: 0-9787875-8-7
ISBN-13: 978-0-9787875-8-5

CONTENTS

Introduction

There are three great books written by prophets that are recognized in Islam. The Quran teaches us that prophethood was given to the sons of Abraham. The Torah was given to Moses, the Injil was given to Jesus, and the Quran was given to Mohammed. In this book, we will study the teachings of these three prophets. We will look at the revelation that each prophet provides, so that we can better understand the ways of God.

Quran 29:27 (Mohsin Khan) And We bestowed on him [Ibrahim (Abraham)], Ishaque (Isaac) and Ya'qub (Jacob), and ordained among his offspring Prophethood and the Book [i.e. the Taurat (Torah) (to Musa - Moses), the Injil (Gospel) (to 'Iesa - Jesus), the Quran (to Muhammad), all from the offspring of Ibrahim (Abraham)], and We granted him his reward in this world, and verily, in the Hereafter he is indeed among the righteous.

Quran 3:3 (Yusufali)
It is He Who sent down to thee (step by step), in truth, the Book, confirming what went before it; and He sent down the Law (of Moses) and the Gospel (of Jesus) before this, as a guide to mankind, and He sent down the criterion (of judgment between right and wrong)

The Quran declares that God sent down the Law of Moses and the Injil. The Quran declares that these writings were given as a guide to mankind. They were not only written to guide the Jews or the Muslims. According to the Quran, they were written to guide all of mankind.

These three great books written by the prophets are part of the foundation upon which a Muslim builds his life. There are six pillars of faith (Iman) found in Islam. These pillars include belief in Allah, belief in *Al-Mala'ika* (the angels), belief in *Ar Rasul* (the messengers), belief in *Al Kutub* (the divine scriptures), belief in *Yawmill Qiyaamah* (the last day) and belief in *Al-Qadar* (the pre-ordained will of God).

If a Muslim desires to build a strong faith in God, he must study the messengers and the revelations that they received. Only then can he build a firm foundation of faith in his life. It is necessary to study the books given to the messengers of God if one wants to have real faith. It is necessary to study the Torah, the Injil, and the Quran if one hopes to discern the difference between real faith in God and false faith.

In this book, we will examine the revelations given to Moses, Jesus and Mohammed, and the books that contain these revelations. If you read this book carefully, you will find the road that leads to salvation.

Many Muslims talk of the errors that are in the Torah and the Injil. Nowhere does the Quran state that these books are full of errors. Is not God able to protect His Scriptures? Is He not able to protect the books that He sends? Men may think that these books are full of errors, but the men who think this way have usually never even read the books that they criticize.

It is true that the Torah and the Injil have been copied, recopied, and translated many times over a period of several thousand years. It is inevitable that when a book is copied, recopied, and translated so many times, small errors will enter the copies. Most of these errors are very minor, such as spelling mistakes and small changes in grammar. Only a few of these errors have caused disagreement among scholars regarding which version of a biblical passage is the correct one.

Nevertheless, the modern versions of these books are extremely accurate. Scholars estimate that the modern version of the Christian Bible is approximately 99 percent accurate. It is far more accurate than the modern versions of other books that have been passed down from the times when the Bible was written.

If you want to build a strong foundation of faith in this life, you must study the Torah and the Injil that are contained in the Christian Bible. If there are errors in these books, surely God will help you to discern what these errors are. But if you never read these books, you will never know what is in them.

In fact, it is necessary to study all three prophets to achieve a better understanding of each individual prophet. If you study the teachings of Moses, you will better understand Jesus and his teachings. If you study the prophecies of Jesus and Moses, you will be able to better understand Mohammed and his revelations.

The first prophet that we will study is Moses. The story of Moses is found in the Torah, together with his teachings and prophecies.

Mohammed, himself, testified about the authority of Moses and the Torah. When a Jewish man and woman were brought to Mohammed because they had committed illegal sexual intercourse, Mohammed asked them "What is the legal punishment for this sin in your book (Torah)?" The Jews tried to hide from Mohammed the penalty for adultery that was written in their own Torah. Mohammed knew better, and the verse of the Torah that condemns adulterers to be stoned to death was read out loud. Mohammed then ordered that the instructions of the Torah, the Law of Moses, should be followed. The man and woman were stoned to death. (Bukhari 8:809)

> Narrated Ibn Umar (RA): A Jew and a Jewess were brought to Allah's Apostle (S) on a charge of committing illegal sexual intercourse. The Prophet asked them: 'What is the legal punishment (for this sin) in your Book (Torah)?' They replied: 'Our priests have innovated the blackening of faces with charcoal and Tajbiya' (being mounted on a donkey, with their faces in opposite directions, then mortified in public). Abdullah bin Salaam said: '0 Allah's Apostle, tell them to bring the Torah.' The Torah was brought, and then one of the Jews put his hand over the Divine Verse of the Rajm (stoning to death) and started reading what preceded and what followed it. On that, Ibn Salaam said to the Jew: 'Lift up your hand.' The Divine Verse of the Rajm was under his hand. So Allah's Apostle (S) ordered that the two (sinners) be stoned to death, and so they were stoned. (Bukhari 8:809)

The second prophet in our study is the prophet Jesus (Isa). Mohammed testified that when a human being is born, Satan touches him on both sides of his body with his two fingers. Mohammed testified that every human being has been touched in this way, except Jesus. Every human being is influenced by evil. Every human being is affected by sin. Except one.

Mohammed testified that Jesus was born of a virgin. A pure and perfect seed was planted in Mary, and Satan was unable to corrupt that seed. Satan was never able to touch Jesus or influence him in any way.

The Quran testifies amazing things about Jesus. Jesus is "Ruhullah", the spirit of God (Quran 21:91) He is the word of God (Quran 3:45). He is Al Masiih (The Messiah). He is righteous. He is holy (Quran 3:42-47). He has power over death (Quran 3:48-54). He raised the dead to life again (Quran 3:49). He gave sight to the blind (Quran 3:49). He healed lepers (Quran 3:49).

The Quran teaches us that Jesus knows the way to heaven and can show us the way (3:55). If you believe the words of the Quran, then you must know that Jesus is a very unique prophet, a prophet who can help you find the way to Paradise. It is my desire that the readers of this book would all find the way to Paradise, where Jesus is (Quran 3:55).

If you want to really know a man, you need to look at where he comes from. You can't really know a man without knowing his family, his background, and his tribe. If we are to know who a prophet is, we must study the prophets who came before him. Their prophecies help us to know the ones who will follow.

The Law was given to Moses, but grace and truth came through Jesus. If we want to know who Mohammed is, we must first study those who came before Mohammed. In Moses, the Law of God revealed the righteousness of God. In Jesus, not only a law was given, but the very Spirit of God was also given. Power was given to keep the Law. If we understand who Moses was, and who Jesus was, then it is possible to understand Mohammed.

In this book, we will study the Law of Moses. Secondly, we will study the life of Jesus. We will look at what the Injil says about Jesus, and at what the Quran says about Jesus. Thirdly, we will study the life of Mohammed.

1 GOD PREPARES MUSA

BLOOD COVENANT

Before we begin with the story of Moses, it is important to understand the concept of a blood covenant. To understand the story of Moses and the story of Jesus, you must understand what a blood covenant is. Blood covenants are found in every religion and in every society. The first mention of a blood covenant is found in the Torah, in the book of Genesis.

The Torah teaches us that in the beginning God created the heavens and the earth. He created the seas and dry land, the birds of the air and the fish of the sea. He created plants and animals. On the sixth day of Creation, God created man in his image, and in his likeness. He said "Let Us make man in Our image, according to Our likeness; let them have dominion over the fish of the sea, over the birds of the air, and over the cattle, over all the earth and over every creeping thing that creeps on the earth" (Genesis 1:26).

And so man was created. He was created to have dominion over the earth, to rule over the earth even as he submitted himself to the Creator.

After creating man, God created woman, from the rib of the first man Adam. As he created woman, God also created something else. He created something known as a blood covenant. It is written in the Torah:

"For this reason a man shall leave his father and his mother, and be joined to his wife; and the two shall become one flesh" (Genesis 2:24).

In a blood covenant, two become one. When a man marries a woman, two become one. When a man marries a woman, they are bound together in covenant. They belong to each other. Their bodies and their possessions belong to each other. This is the power of the blood covenant, in which two become one.

When a woman has sexual intercourse with a man for the first time, there is blood. Why did God create the body in this way? This blood is a sign from God that a blood covenant is being formed, that two people are becoming one. In marriage, this is a good thing, as a man and his wife are joined together in covenant.

The devil knows that man was created to rule the earth. The devil and his evil spirits desired to rule the earth in the place of man. The devil knows that the only way he can rule over the earth and over mankind is if he can trick man into forming a blood covenant with him. If the devil is able to trick men into forming a blood covenant, then two become one. Everything that a man has then becomes the possession of his covenant partner. All the authority that God gave to man is then given to the devil. Man was created to rule the earth, but if he forms a covenant with the devil, then the devil is given the right to rule the earth.

The devil knows how to trick people into forming blood covenants with him so that they are joined to him. In this way, everything a man has comes under the ownership and control of the devil.

This is why idolatry is such a terrible sin. Idols represent the devil and his evil spirits. When men worship idols, they make animal sacrifices to those idols. As they offer these sacrifices of blood to idols, they form blood covenants with the evil spirits that are represented by those idols.

When you read the Torah, you read about temples built to worship the idols of Baal. When a man wished to worship Baal, he went to the temple of Baal. Large feasts were held in the temple of Baal. Goats and other animals would be sacrificed to Baal. Then, everyone would eat the meat of those goats in the feasts that were held in Baal's temple. As the people ate the meat of those goats, they formed a blood covenant with Baal. In a blood covenant, two become one. As they ate the meat of that goat, the people gave themselves to Baal. They became the people of Baal, and Baal became their god.

The temples of Baal also had temple prostitutes. When men worshiped Baal, they went to the temple and slept with the prostitute of the temple. As they did so, they formed a blood covenant with the evil spirits of Baal, who was represented by those prostitutes.

Do you understand why the worship of idols is such a terrible sin? It is impossible to be a true worshiper of God when one forms blood covenants with the devil and his evil spirits. It is impossible to worship both God and the devil. The one who worships idols belongs to the devil.

ABRAHAM'S COVENANT WITH GOD

When Abraham was 99 years old, God appeared to him and said "I am Almighty God, walk before Me and be blameless. And I will make My covenant between Me and you, and will multiply you exceedingly…. Behold, My covenant is with you and you shall be a father of many nations….This is My covenant which you shall keep, between Me and you and your descendants after you: Every male child among you shall be circumcised" (Genesis 17:1,2,4,10).

This is the covenant that God made with Abraham. In this covenant, Abraham and his descendants were circumcised. As the blood of circumcision flowed, Abraham and his sons, Ishmael and Isaac, entered into a blood covenant with the true God. In a covenant, two become one. In this covenant, Abraham and his sons became the people of God, the people connected by blood covenant to God. In this covenant, God became the God of Abraham. Even today, we know the true God by the name *The God of Abraham*, the God who made covenant with Abraham.

When God deals with man, he does so through covenant. Without a covenant, man could never come before God. Without a covenant, man has no right to come before God. God is holy, and man is a sinner. Man's sin keeps him from having the right to come to God. But when God makes a blood covenant with man, he takes away man's sin and makes it possible for a man to come to God. This is the power of covenant.

As we read the stories, teachings, and prophecies of Moses and Jesus, we will be studying the covenants that God made with man. God made a blood covenant with Abraham and his sons, the sign of which was circumcision. The followers of Jesus also enter into a blood covenant with God, a new and better covenant. In this book we will discuss the covenants that make it possible for men to become the children of God.

THE ISRAELITES COME TO EGYPT

Abraham lived in the land of Canaan, where he raised his sons, Ishmael and Isaac. Isaac was the father of Jacob, who is also known as Israel. The descendants of Israel are often referred to in the Torah as the "Children of Israel", or Israelites.

Jacob had twelve sons. One of his sons was Joseph. The brothers of Joseph were jealous of him because he was the favorite son of his father. Their resentment towards Joseph became so great that they decided to get rid of him. Joseph's brothers sold Joseph into slavery and told his father that wild animals had eaten him.

Joseph became a slave in Egypt. Yet, even as a slave, God helped Joseph. Joseph had the ability to interpret dreams. When the Pharaoh of Egypt received a dream that troubled him, Joseph told him what the dream meant. He told the Pharaoh that seven years of famine were coming to Egypt, and that the Egyptians needed to prepare for the famine.

The Pharaoh listened to Joseph, and prepared for the famine. Joseph became the top administrator in the land of Egypt, as he worked to store up grain for the famine. When the famine arrived, the Egyptians had stored up plenty of grain. Meanwhile, in the land of Canaan, Joseph's family suffered under the famine. Finally, Isaac sent Joseph's brothers to Egypt to try to buy food from the Pharaoh.

Joseph was the one who met his brothers in Egypt. After he revealed his identity to them, he forgave his brothers and gave them food. He invited them to come to Egypt where there was plenty of food. And so the family moved to Egypt, where Joseph cared for them.

The Israelites multiplied and prospered in Egypt. Four hundred years passed, and the Israelites became a mighty nation within the land of Egypt. Some of

The Law of God and the Prophets of Islam

the Egyptians began to resent the Israelites, because of the way they multiplied and prospered. Eventually, a king came to power in Egypt who turned against the Israelites and forced them work as slaves.

Even after the Israelites were forced to become slaves, it seemed like God's blessing was on them. The Israelites continued to multiply at a rapid rate, until the Egyptians began to fear that the Israelites might soon outnumber them in their own land. Pharaoh, the king of Egypt, gave a terrible order. He commanded the Israelite midwives to murder every male child that was born to an Israelite mother.

The midwives feared God and disobeyed the order. When Pharaoh discovered that male children were still being born to the children of Israel, he became enraged and ordered his soldiers to kill every male child of Israel.

THE BIRTH OF MOSES

An Israelite woman conceived and gave birth to a son during this time. His name was Moses. The mother of Moses knew that the soldiers were searching for male children to murder. So she made a small boat out of reeds, and covered the boat with asphalt and pitch. She put her child in the small boat and floated the boat among the reeds that grew at the edge of the Nile River, safely out of sight.

One of Pharaoh's daughters came down to the river to bathe, together with the maids that served her. As she was bathing, she saw the small boat floating among the reeds. Curiosity overtook her, and she ordered one of her maids to bring her the small boat. When she peered inside, she saw baby Moses.

Pharaoh's daughter had a compassionate heart. When she saw the newborn baby, she immediately turned her heart towards the child. She knew that her father had ordered all Hebrew babies to be killed, but she decided to use her position to make an exception for this child. She decided to raise the child as her own.

And so Moses was raised by the daughter of Pharaoh. Pharaoh's daughter needed someone to nurse and care for the child. One of her maids found a mother who had milk, a mother who could nurse and care for Moses. The

13

mother found by the maid was actually Moses' real mother. His own mother nursed him, but he was the adopted son of Pharaoh's daughter.

Moses was raised as a prince of Egypt in the palace of the Pharaoh. Moses learned all the wisdom and knowledge of the Egyptians. He learned the ways of the palace. He learned about the idols and gods of the Egyptians. At the same time, his real mother taught him about the one true God, the God of Abraham. When Moses came of age, he made a choice. He chose to be an Israelite instead of an Egyptian. He chose to follow the God of his forefather, Abraham. He chose to enter into covenant with the true God instead of worshiping the idols and false gods of Egypt.

MOSES FLEES EGYPT

Moses lived in the palace, but the Israelites suffered as slaves in Egypt. One day, Moses saw an Egyptian man beating an Israelite slave. Moses decided to take action. He could not bear to see one of his Israelite brothers beaten in such a cruel manner. Moses was a strong man, given the very best military training that the Egyptians could offer. He grabbed the Egyptian by the throat, choked him to death, and buried the body in the sand. He hoped that nobody knew what he had done.

The next day, as Moses walked among the Israelites, he saw two Israelite slaves fighting with each other. Moses intervened and said to one of the men "Why are you striking your companion?"

The slaves answered Moses rudely saying, "Who made you the judge over us? Are you going to kill us like you killed that Egyptian yesterday?"

Moses was shocked. Fear gripped him. He knew that people were talking about the Egyptian he had killed the day before. He knew that the Pharaoh would soon hear the story and would know that Moses had decided to be an Israelite instead of an Egyptian. Pharaoh would know that Moses had decided to follow the God of Israel, instead of the gods and idols of the Egyptians.

In fear for his life, Moses fled from Egypt and entered the barren desert of Midian. In the desert, Moses became exhausted and desperate for something to drink. Finally, he found a well of water. After drinking, he sat down on the ground by the well.

A Midianite man named Reuel had seven daughters. These young women brought their father's sheep to the well to water them. As they were drawing up the water and filling the water troughs, some shepherds came and began to chase them away. When Moses saw that the young women were in trouble, he stood up and confronted the shepherds. The shepherds feared this strange Egyptian man, and they fled. Moses helped the women water their sheep.

The women returned home to their father. The father was surprised that they were home so early, because the shepherds usually made it very difficult for his daughters to water their flock. He asked them, "How is it that you have come so soon today?" The daughters answered, "An Egyptian delivered us from the hand of the shepherds and helped us to water their flock." Then Reuel said "And where is he? Why did you leave him alone in the desert? Call him to come and eat with us."

And so Moses came to the home of Reuel. He ended up staying with that family, working as a shepherd. Eventually Reuel gave his daughter, Zipporah, to Moses as a wife.

Moses went from being a favored prince in the most powerful empire of the world, to being a shepherd in the desert. Instead of dealing with the political issues of the Egyptian empire, Moses' life revolved around taking care of a few dozen sheep in the desert. He spent his days searching for sufficient grass and water to care for them in that barren place.

Years passed, and Moses became an old man. At the age of eighty, Moses was still taking care of sheep in the desert. Pharaoh's palace was just a distant memory. Moses was just a shepherd.

Even though it seemed that Moses had failed in life, his real calling still lay ahead of him. Before a prophet can be sent by God, it is very important that the prophet learns humility. Moses was an arrogant prince of Egypt. In the desert he learned humility.

Now Moses was an old man, a broken man. He was no longer a prince. He was just a shepherd. Moses was no longer confident in his strength, because the strength of his youth had faded. He was no longer confident in his wisdom, because his ideas had failed him. When Moses attacked and killed the Egyptian, he thought that the children of Abraham would follow him as

15

their leader. Instead, they had rejected him and mocked him, forcing him to flee to the desert.

You see, a true prophet of God must not be arrogant. If a prophet is arrogant, he will begin to add his own words to God's words. He will begin to confuse his own desires and thoughts with God's desires and thoughts. He will begin to prophesy things that God has not actually spoken. He will begin to speak prophecies that benefit himself, instead of prophecies that are actually from God.

An arrogant prophet might say that God told him that the people should give him money. An arrogant prophesy might prophesy that God told him to take another man's wife. An arrogant prophet becomes a false prophet, because he adds his own words to God's words.

MOSES MEETS THE TRUE GOD

One day as Moses walked through the desert, he saw an amazing sight. A bush was blazing with fire, and yet the bush did not burn up. Moses was very curious. And as he approached the bush a voice spoke to him, "Moses, Moses!"

Moses was terrified and spoke the only words he could think of: "Here I am."

The voice continued, "Do not draw near this place. Take your sandals off your feet, for the place where you stand is holy ground."

"I am the God of your father—the God of Abraham, the God of Isaac, and the God of Jacob."

"I have surely seen the oppression of My people who are in Egypt and have heard their cry because of their slave masters. I know their sorrows. I have come down to deliver them out of the hand of the Egyptians, and to bring them up from that land to a good and large land, to a land flowing with milk and honey."

A terrible fear gripped Moses and he hid his face from the awesome presence of God. In that moment Moses knew that he was in the presence of the Creator, the one who formed heaven and earth with His word. In that moment, Moses knew that God was holy and that he was not. He felt terribly insecure as he became aware of his own uncleanness and sin. The memories of his sins and foolish words flashed through his mind.

THE HOLINESS OF GOD

This is what happens when mere men encounter the true and living God. They become aware of the awesome holiness of God, and they become aware of their own sinfulness. They know that unless God extends His mercy to them, they will be instantly destroyed.

When Adam and Eve were created, there were given a simple instruction. "Of every tree of the garden you may freely eat; but of the tree of the knowledge of good and evil you shall not eat, for in the day that you eat of it you shall surely die."

From the beginning, the price of sin was death. When Adam and Eve disobeyed God and ate from the tree of the knowledge of good and evil, they immediately knew that they were sinners who deserved to die. When God came looking for them in the garden, they hid from Him, terrified because of their sins, and ashamed of their nakedness. They tried to cover their nakedness with clothes made from fig leaves.

When God found Adam and Eve hiding from Him, He did not kill them immediately. He gave them clothes made of animal skins to cover their nakedness. As they wore these skins, Adam and Eve knew that those animals died because of their sin. The price of sin is death.

When Adam and Eve sinned, sin and death entered this world. From that moment on, sin has spread like poison through the entire human race. From that moment on, men began to die as death worked in their bodies, decaying their flesh. A man's body lives only a few years, until death overtakes him.

God is holy. His holiness is like a burning fire. He is without sin, without imperfection. When a sinful person comes into the presence of the Holy One, that person knows in his heart that he is a sinner. When that sinful person comes into the presence of the Holy One, he knows in his heart that the penalty of sin is death. This penalty for sin was spoken to our father Adam, and every man remembers this penalty when he meets the living God.

This is why mere men fall on their faces like dead men when they meet the living God. The Lord's presence is like a consuming fire. He is so pure and so powerful, that mere men cannot stand before Him. It is only His mercy and grace that allows any person to continue to live in His presence.

GOD SENDS MOSES

God spoke to Moses from the burning bush and told him what he needed to do. He said, "Come now, and I will send you to Pharaoh, the king of Egypt, so that you may bring My people, the children of Israel, out of Egypt."

For many years, the Lord had listened to the prayers of the children of Abraham as they suffered as slaves in Egypt. It was now time for those prayers to be answered. It was time for the Israelites to be delivered out of the hand of Pharaoh. It was time for judgment to come upon the idol worshipers of Egypt. It was a time of liberty for the people of God.

Moses' heart was full of doubt, and he began to question God. He asked, "When I go to Pharaoh, whom shall I say has sent me?"

God answered, "Tell Pharaoh that 'I AM who I AM.' Say to the children of Israel, 'I AM has sent me to you.' "

God continued, "Tell the children of Israel that the God of Abraham, the God of Isaac, and the God of Jacob has sent you to them. Tell them that God has seen their suffering in Egypt, and that He will bring them out of Egypt and bring them to a land flowing with milk and honey. They will listen to you. Then take the elders of Israel to the Pharaoh and tell Pharaoh to allow you to journey into the wilderness for three days to worship God in the wilderness. Pharaoh will refuse to let you journey into the wilderness to worship me, and I will stretch out my hand against Pharaoh. I will strike Egypt with wonders, and after that he will let you go."

THE SIGNS OF A PROPHET

Moses didn't think he could possibly stand before Pharaoh and demand that he free the slaves. He didn't even think the Israelites would listen to him or receive him as their leader. The last time he had tried to fight for the Israelites, things ended in disaster. Moses disputed with the Lord, saying, "What if the Israelites don't believe me or listen to me? What if they say, 'The Lord has not appeared to you?'"

The Lord answered Moses with an unusual question. "What is in your hand?" He asked Moses.

Moses was holding a shepherd's rod that he used to herd his sheep. Moses looked at his rod, and answered, "A rod." God said to Moses, "Throw your rod on the ground." Moses obeyed. As soon the rod struck the ground, it became a hissing snake. Moses reacted in terror and fled from the snake.

Then God said "Reach out your hand and pick up the snake by the tail. Although he was still trembling with fear, Moses did so. Immediately, the snake became his shepherd's rod once again.

In this way God gave Moses a mighty sign to convince the children of Israel that God had sent him. Prophets who are sent from God are not sent empty-handed. They are sent with power. They are sent with supernatural signs from God.

When a prophet is sent from God, he does not trust in his own strength. He must trust in the one who sends him. He must trust in the living God. He does not trust in the strength of a human army. He trusts in the supernatural power of God.

All through the Torah and the Injil, we read of prophets who performed great signs so that their followers would know they were sent from God. The prophet Elijah called fire down from heaven and performed great miracles when he confronted the idol worshipers. One time an entire army of idol worshipers was struck blind when Elijah prophesied against them. The prophet Isaiah prophesied against the king of Assyria, and 180,000 Assyrians were struck dead by the hand of God. Jesus raised the dead, opened the eyes of the blind, and performed many great miracles.

Even after Moses had received the great sign of the snake, he continued to be full of doubt. He began to argue with God, explaining to God why he could not obey Him. Moses said, "O my Lord, I am not eloquent…. I am slow of speech and slow of tongue."

The Lord rebuked Moses and asked him, "Who has made man's mouth? Have not I, the Lord?"

As Moses argued with God, the anger of the Lord began to grow. Finally, the Lord agreed to allow Moses to take his brother, Aaron, with him when he went to speak to Pharaoh. Moses would tell Aaron what to say, and Aaron would do the talking.

The Lord concluded his instructions to Moses. He said to him, "Tell Pharaoh this: 'Israel is my son, my firstborn. If you refuse to release the children of Israel from their slavery, I will kill your son, your firstborn.'"

ZIPPORAH SAVES MOSES

After the encounter, Moses walked back to his camp. The Lord was angry with Moses because Moses continued to doubt the word of God even after God had demonstrated his great power to Moses. When Moses argued with God, he showed that he was rebellious against the will of God.

The rebellion of Moses against God can be seen in another way. Moses had never circumcised his son. The children of Israel were supposed to walk in covenant with God. The sign of this covenant, given to their father Abraham, was circumcision. All the Israelites were supposed to be circumcised as a sign that they belonged to God, and that He belonged to them. Circumcision was a blood covenant between the children of Abraham and God.

Moses was a prophet of God, sent to speak the word of God to Pharaoh. He was sent to warn Pharaoh that out of all the nations, the children of Israel were God's firstborn son. If Pharaoh refused to release God's firstborn son Israel from slavery, God would kill the firstborn sons of Egypt.

To speak a warning such as this one is very dangerous. There is a principal found in the Torah and in the Injil: judgment begins in the house of the Lord. Before God judges evildoers, He must first judge His own people. If a prophet is sent to speak a word of judgment, he must know that he will also be judged. A prophet must not be a hypocrite. If a prophet calls people to repent of idolatry, and that prophet is himself an idol worshiper, he will be the first one to be judged by God.

Moses never circumcised his sons. He never brought his own sons into the blood covenant with the living God. He did not teach his sons the ways of God. And now he was being sent to speak the word of God to Pharaoh and to teach the Israelites the ways of God.

As he walked back to the camp, God's anger burned against Moses. As he approached his camp, the Lord met him and was about to kill him.

Moses' wife, Zipporah, saw what was happening. She knew her husband was about to be killed. She understood the sin of Moses. She understood his hypocrisy, that he had not obeyed the commands of God, although he was about to declare God's judgment to Pharaoh.

Zipporah jumped into action. She took a knife and circumcised their son and threw the foreskin before the feet of Moses. She cried out "Surely you are a husband of blood to me!"

When Zipporah did this act, she was reminding God of his covenant with the children of Israel. She was reminding God that her family belonged to the living God, that they had a blood covenant with God. As she did this she declared that Moses was her husband by blood. In other words, she and Moses were united by the blood covenant of marriage. They were one. Therefore, if God wanted to kill Moses, she must also be killed. And if God wanted to show mercy to Zipporah because of the act of obedience that she demonstrated when she circumcised her son, then God must also show mercy to Moses.

God honored the action of Zipporah and showed mercy to her and to Moses. The life of Moses was spared. When God's anger against sin is about to break out against a man, the only thing that will save that man is a blood covenant between God and man.

And so, Moses lived, and learned to fear the Lord. He never again argued with the Lord in such a rebellious manner. From that day on, he taught his sons and his followers the ways of the Lord. He learned true humility in the sight of God.

MOSES AND AARON CONFRONT PHARAOH

Moses met with his brother Aaron and told him all the words that the Lord had given him. Moses and Aaron gathered the elders of the children of Israel. Aaron spoke to the elders everything that Moses told him to speak. Moses performed the signs that God had given him in the sight of all the people. When the people saw the signs, they believed. When they heard that God had listened to their prayers and looked upon their suffering, they bowed their heads and worshiped God.

Afterwards, Moses and Aaron went to meet with Pharaoh. Aaron said to Pharaoh, "Thus says the Lord God of Israel: 'Let My people go, so that they can hold a feast to Me in the wilderness.'"

Pharaoh was not impressed with the demands of Aaron and Moses. He answered rudely, "Who is the Lord, that I should obey his voice to let Israel go? I do not know the Lord, nor will I let Israel go."

Pharaoh accused Moses and Aaron of helping the slaves escape from their work. He accused the slaves of being lazy. He decided to increase the work that the slaves needed to do. Instead of providing the slaves with straw to make bricks, he told them that now they must provide their own straw, and yet produce just as many bricks as before.

As the Israelites suffered under their increased workload, they became angry with Moses. They blamed him for going to Pharaoh with his demands and angering Pharaoh. Now Moses was completely alone. He called out to God in his distress, saying "God, why did you send me to Pharaoh? He has not freed the Israelites. He has become even worse than before!"

The Lord answered Moses. He reminded Moses that he was the God of Abraham, Isaac and Jacob. He reminded Moses that the children of Israel were His people, and He was their God. He told Moses that he heard the cries of the Israelites and knew their suffering.

He said to Moses: "I am the LORD; I will bring you out from under the burdens of the Egyptians, I will rescue you from their bondage, and I will redeem you with an outstretched arm and with great judgments. I will take you as My people, and I will be your God. Then you shall know that I am the LORD your God who brings you out from under the burdens of the Egyptians. And I will bring you into the land which I swore to give to

Abraham, Isaac, and Jacob; and I will give it to you as a heritage: I am the LORD."

The Lord told Moses to go back to Pharaoh to speak to him again. This time, the Lord told Moses that when Pharaoh questioned him, he was to cast his rod upon the ground.

And so, Moses and Aaron went to Pharaoh once again. Once again, they demanded that the children of Israel should be let go. Once again, Pharaoh reacted rudely. He said to them "What miracle can you show me to prove that God has sent you?"

When Pharaoh said this, Aaron cast down his rod in front of Pharaoh. Immediately, the rod became a serpent. Pharaoh was shocked by the snake, but he wasn't willing to admit that this snake was a sign from the true God. He decided to prove that the false gods and idols of Egypt were as powerful as God. He called his sorcerers, so that they could imitate the sign that Moses had displayed.

The sorcerers of Egypt gathered, and they called upon their spirits and their jinn. They threw their sticks to the ground, and amazingly enough, their sticks were changed into snakes also. As everyone watched, something extraordinary happened. The snake that came from Moses staff swallowed up the snakes that were created by the magicians of the Pharaoh. Satan and the jinn are able to perform certain kinds of miracles, but the miracles that come from the true God will always be greater.

Pharaoh refused to admit that God's power was greater than the power of his magicians. He hardened his heart and refused to set the Israelites free. In fact, it was God Himself who hardened Pharaoh's heart. God wanted to demonstrate His greatness before all Egypt. As Pharaoh's heart was hardened, great and terrible judgments were released upon the land of Egypt.

The next morning, Moses met Pharaoh as Pharaoh came down to the River Nile. Once again, Moses and Aaron spoke the word of the Lord to Pharaoh, ordering him to let the children of Israel go. Then Aaron raised up his rod and struck the waters of the Nile River. Immediately, the waters of the Nile were turned into blood. All the water of the Egyptians, in ponds, streams, and drinking containers were turned into blood. The fish died and the people had nothing to drink.

Even as Pharaoh witnessed this great and terrible miracle, his heart was not moved. He called his magicians to see if they were able to perform a similar sign. The magicians were able to turn some water into something that looked like blood. When Pharaoh saw signs performed by his own magicians, he hardened his heart and refused to let the children of Israel go.

After seven days had passed Moses and Aaron again went up to Pharaoh to speak the word of the Lord. This time the Lord said, "Let my people go that they may serve me. But if you refuse to let them go, I will smite all your territory with frogs."

Aaron stretched out his rod over the Nile River, and frogs immediately began to leave the Nile River by the millions to invade the homes of the Egyptians. Once again, Pharaoh tried to show that his magicians could perform a similar sign. When Pharaoh asked them, the magicians of Egypt were able to cause some frogs to leave the water and hop up onto dry land. Of course, the last thing Egypt needed was for more frogs to leave the rivers! The people were already suffering from the over-abundance of frogs.

Pharaoh finally asked Moses to remove the frogs, promising him that if he did so, the children of Israel would be released from their slavery so that they could worship God in the desert. In response to Pharaoh's promise, Moses told Pharaoh to tell him the exact hour when he wanted the frogs to die. At that hour, Moses prayed to God, and immediately the frogs died. The Egyptians gathered them into great stinking heaps.

Pharaoh did not keep his promise. After the frogs had died, he refused to release the Israelites from their bondage. Therefore, the judgments of God continued to be released upon Egypt.

The Lord ordered Aaron to stretch out his rod and to strike the dust of the ground. As he struck the dust, the dust became lice. The lice spread throughout the land of Egypt in great clouds. Every man and every animal was covered in lice.

Pharaoh called his magicians to see if they too could create lice. This time, the magicians told Pharaoh that this miracle was too much for them. They were unable to imitate this miracle. The magicians of Egypt only had limited power at their command. They did not have the unlimited power of the Creator working through them. They only had the power of Satan and the jinn. They could change the form of something, but they could not create living things. They told Pharaoh: "This is not mere magic. This is the finger of God."

Pharaoh refused to listen to his magicians or to Moses. He refused to release the Israelites from their bondage. So Moses stood before Pharaoh once again as he took his morning bath in the Nile. He said to Pharaoh, "Let my people go that they may serve me!"

Pharaoh refused once again. This time the Lord sent thick swarms of flies into the house of Pharaoh and into all the homes of the Egyptians. The flies did not enter the homes of the Israelites.

Pharaoh called Moses and Aaron and told them that they could enter the desert with the Israelites if they would pray for the plague of flies to be lifted. So Moses prayed, and immediately, the flies disappeared. Not one remained. As soon as the flies were no more, Pharaoh hardened his heart and refused to release the Israelites.

And so the plagues continued. A severe disease destroyed the animals of the Egyptians, without touching the animals owned by the Israelites. A plague of painful sores and boils came upon the Egyptians, and upon Pharaoh himself. A plague of hail destroyed the crops of the Egyptians and killed all the livestock that were in the fields. A plague of locusts destroyed every green thing that escaped the hail. After each plague, Pharaoh hardened his heart and refused to set the Israelites free.

The Egyptians themselves began to beg Pharaoh to release the Israelites. They said "Please, Pharaoh, let these people go. Don't you see that Egypt is being destroyed?" But Pharaoh refused.

The ninth plague to fall upon Egypt was a plague of darkness. Moses stretched his hands to heaven, and darkness came upon Egypt. It was such a deep darkness that people could actually feel the darkness. For three days no Egyptian could leave his home or even see his hand in front of his face. At the same time, the children of Israel had light in their homes.

With each plague, God demonstrated his superiority over the false gods and idols of Egypt. The Egyptians worshiped the Nile River. That river was turned to blood. The Egyptians worshiped the sun. The sun was turned to darkness. The false gods of Egypt were brought low as the judgments of the true God came upon Egypt.

Even after the terrifying experience of the sun turning to darkness, Pharaoh refused to release the Israelites. When Moses spoke with Pharaoh after this plague, Pharaoh hardened his heart even more than before. He told Moses that he would never see his face again. He warned Moses, "Get away from me! Be careful that you never see my face again! If you ever see my face again, you will die!"

Moses replied "You have spoken well. I will never see your face again."

THE BLOOD OF A LAMB

As Pharaoh rejected the word of the Lord for the final time, he rejected the opportunity to receive mercy instead of judgment. Now, the worst judgment of all was released upon Egypt. Every family of Israel was instructed by God how to escape the coming judgment. Each Israelite family was instructed to choose a perfect, year-old male lamb and to sacrifice that lamb to the Lord. Each family was told to roast that lamb and eat it with herbs and unleavened bread. They were told to be dressed for a long journey as they ate the lamb. Most importantly, each family was told to take the blood of the lamb and to place it above their door, and on the doorposts on each side of the door. The blood of the lamb would protect them from the terrible judgment of the Lord that was about to come.

The Israelites obeyed the word of the Lord. Each family chose a perfect male lamb. Each family dressed for a journey. Each family slaughtered its lamb and ate the roasted meat and placed the blood of the lamb upon their doorposts.

That night, a great tragedy came upon the Egyptians, as the angel of the Lord visited every home in Egypt. When the angel saw the blood of the Lamb upon the doorposts of an Israelite home, he "passed over" that home, without harming any of the inhabitants of that home. When the Lord came to a home where the blood of the Lamb was absent, He took the life of the firstborn son of that family. Every Egyptian family was struck by this judgment, from the family of the prisoner in the dungeon to the family of the Pharaoh himself.

When the holy God visits a nation of idol worshipers and sinners, what do you think will happen? The true God is a holy fire. Moses was instructed not to come too close to that fire, or he would die. When the angel of the Lord visited the homes of the Egyptian idol worshipers, many lost their lives.

The only thing that could save life on that night was the blood of a lamb. This lamb is called the "Passover" lamb, because when the Lord saw the blood of that lamb He "passed over" that home and that home was not judged. When the Lord saw the blood of the lamb, he remembered the blood covenant that connected the Israelites to Him.

As morning approached, the Egyptians discovered that death had visited every one of their homes. A great cry rose out of the land of Egypt, as the Egyptians mourned their dead.

When Pharaoh saw what had happened, he cried out to the Israelites "Rise, go out from among my people, both you and the children of Israel. And go, serve the LORD as you have said! Take your flocks and your herds, and be gone!" The Egyptian people also begged the Israelites to leave their land. They feared that if the Israelites stayed, every Egyptian would lose his life.

And so the Israelites were delivered out of Egypt. A great multitude of Israelites left Egypt in the early hours of the morning and entered the desert.

THE RED SEA

Pharaoh hardened his heart a final time. After the Israelites left his nation, he decided that he could simply not tolerate the loss of his slaves. Pharaoh was an extremely arrogant man, a man worshiped as a god. He could not allow these slaves to defeat him and his nation. So, he gathered his troops and followed the Israelites into the desert.

The Israelites traveled for several days, until they came to the Red Sea. At the Red Sea, they could not continue going forward. Meanwhile, the army of Egypt was approaching. The army of Pharaoh was the most powerful military force of that time. The soldiers of Pharaoh were equipped with the best weapons of their day, including horses and chariots, while most of the Israelites were unarmed. The Red Sea was in front of them, and the army of Pharaoh was behind them, cutting off any escape. The Israelites were trapped. It seemed like they were about to be slaughtered by the idol worshipers.

In fact, it was the army of the Egyptians that was about to be destroyed. That night, God placed a pillar of fire between the Israelites and the army of Pharaoh. This pillar of fire was the fire of God. It was the fire that brings judgment upon the enemies of God. The Israelites were kept safe throughout the night because the Egyptians were afraid to approach the fire.

The next day, the Lord spoke to Moses and told him to stretch out his staff over the Red Sea. As he did so, a great wind began to blow. The wind blew throughout the night, and the waters began to separate from one another until a pathway of dry land stretched into the sea. Moses and the Israelites crossed the Red Sea on dry land, as the pillar of fire kept the Egyptians from approaching.

When all the Israelites had crossed the Red Sea, the pillar of fire disappeared as the morning light dawned. Pharaoh and his armies saw the last of the Israelites crossing over the Red Sea onto the shore at the other side. Pharaoh seized the opportunity. He commanded his soldiers to follow the Israelites, following the same path that crossed the Red Sea that the Israelites had taken. When all the Egyptian soldiers had entered the path that crossed the Red Sea, Moses stretched his hand over the sea once again, and the waters returned to their full depth. The soldiers and horses of Pharaoh were all drowned in the sea as the waters returned.

The children of Israel rejoiced! God had rescued them. Miriam, the sister of Moses, led the Israelites in singing a song of praise to the Lord:

> "I will sing to the Lord, for He is highly exalted.
> Both horse and driver He has hurled into the sea.
> The Lord is my strength and my defense;
> He has become my salvation.
>
> He is my God, and I will praise Him,
> My father's God, and I will exalt Him.
> The Lord is a warrior;
> The Lord is His name.
> Pharaoh's chariots and his army
> He has hurled into the sea…"

LESSONS FROM THE STORY OF MOSES

What can we learn from the story of Moses and the deliverance of the Israelites? We learn how God prepares a prophet. A prophet must understand that he cannot mix his own words with God's words. A prophet must be a humble man who has learned to fear the Lord.

We also learn that God does not send a prophet empty-handed. God gives His prophets great and mighty signs that the devil is unable to duplicate. The power of God is much, much greater than the power of a jinn or an evil spirit.

We learn from this story that God is holy, and that His anger burns against disobedience, rebellion, and idolatry. The judgment of God is especially severe for those who are sent by God. The man who is sent to speak the words of God must walk in humility and obedience, or he might be destroyed. God is a holy, consuming fire, and those who walk with God are walking close to this fire. They must walk carefully. Moses almost died because of his rebellion and disobedience when he met with God.

In the Quran Mohammed testifies about what would happen to him if he spoke something false about Allah:

> And if he (Muhammad) had forged a false saying concerning Us We surely should have seized him by his right hand (or with power and might), and then certainly should have cut off his life artery (Aorta). (Quran 69:44-46, Hilali-Khan)

When the Lord comes with judgment, a man cannot trust in his own righteousness. He cannot think that because he is just as good as his neighbors, he won't be affected by God's judgment. Only one thing can save a man when the Lord comes to judge. The only thing that can save a man when God comes in judgment is a blood covenant with God. When Moses was about to be killed by God, Zipporah circumcised her son, and reminded God of the blood covenant that Abraham and his children had with God.

And when the angel of the Lord came to bring God's judgment to the homes of the Egyptians, it was the blood of a perfect, male lamb that saved the Israelites from destruction. The blood of a lamb speaks of the blood covenant that the Lord makes with true believers in him. We will speak more of this blood covenant in the last part of this book. There is a very special covenant that God makes with His people that comes through the blood of a perfect lamb.

The blood of the lamb also speaks about the price of sin. From the beginning, the price of sin was death. When Adam and Eve ate the fruit of the tree of the knowledge of good and evil, sin and death entered this world.

THE ISRAELITES LEARN TO KNOW GOD IN THE WILDERNESS

After the Israelites escaped from Pharaoh and his army, they entered the wilderness. God did not immediately allow the children of Israel to enter the land of Canaan that He had promised them. Before they entered the good land of their forefather Abraham, God taught them His ways in the wilderness.

You see, the Israelites did not really know God. They had lived as slaves in Egypt for so long that they had forgotten many things about the God of Abraham. They had lived for a long time among the idol worshipers of Egypt. In fact, they knew more about the false gods of Egypt than they knew about the true God. In the desert, the Israelites learned to know their God.

In the desert the Israelites learned to know God as the Provider. In the desert, there was no food. Every morning, bread known as manna fell from heaven. Every morning the Israelites only needed to go outside and gather up this miracle bread to feed their families. The Israelites never went hungry during their years in the desert. When the Israelites became thirsty, God ordered Moses to strike a rock. When he did so, water gushed out of the rock, enough water to satisfy the entire nation. When the Israelites complained about not having meat to eat, God caused millions of quail to be driven by the winds right to the Israelite campsite. God provided all the needs of the Israelites while they were in the desert. Even their clothes and their shoes never wore out during the years they traveled through the desert.

In the desert, the Israelites learned to know God as the Healer. Sickness and disease do not come from God. There is no sickness or disease in heaven, or in the Garden of Eden. Sickness and disease come because of sin, because man does not walk close to God. The Egyptians suffered under many diseases because of their idolatry and other sins. When the Israelites entered the desert, God promised them, "If you diligently heed the voice of the LORD your God and do what is right in His sight …I will put none of the diseases on you which I have brought on the Egyptians. For I am the LORD who heals you (Jehovah-Rapha) ."

Vaughn Martin

2 The Ten Commandments

In the desert, the Israelites also learned about the righteousness of God. In the desert God gave Moses the Law. In its shortened form, Christians and Jews sometimes refer to this law as the Ten Commandments.

These are the Ten Commandments in shortened form that are revered by Christians, Jews and Muslims:

1) You shall have no other gods before Me.
2) You shall not make for yourself an idol.
3) You shall not take the name of the LORD your God in vain.
4) Remember the Sabbath day, to keep it holy.
5) Honor your father and mother, that your days may be long.
6) You shall not murder.
7) You shall not commit adultery.
8) You shall not steal.
9) You shall not bear false witness against your neighbor.
10) You shall not covet.

The Law of Moses included many other instructions and commands that revealed the righteousness of God, but these Ten Commandments are a central part of the Law of Moses. These Ten Commandments were written by God on tablets of stone. These tablets were given to Moses when God met with him on Mount Sinai.

TWO TERRIBLE THINGS ABOUT THE LAW

The Law of Moses seemed like a good opportunity for people to follow God. It seemed like a simple plan that a man could follow so that he could enter heaven. Everyone wants to enter heaven. Everyone wants to avoid the fire of hell.

Unfortunately, the Law of Moses is not an easy law to keep. There are two extremely difficult things that one needs to know about this law. First of all, if you break one part of the law, you break all of it. Secondly, the price of breaking the law is death.

IF YOU BREAK ONE PART OF THE LAW, YOU BREAK ALL OF IT

If you break one part of the law, you break all of it. Moses wrote "Cursed is he who does not confirm the words of this law by doing them."

In the Christian scriptures it is written this way: "All who rely on observing the law are under a curse, for it is written 'Cursed is everyone who does not continue to do everything written in the book of the law'" (Galatians 3:10).

The Law of Moses will not help you if you keep only 50 percent of this law. Neither will it help you if you keep 95 percent of this law. The only person who is declared innocent by the Law of Moses is the person who keeps 100 percent of this law. The man who breaks one of the commandments of the Law of Moses is guilty of breaking the entire law.

James, one of the apostles of Jesus, wrote it this way: "Whoever shall keep the whole law, and yet stumble in one point, he is guilty of all. For He who said,

'Do not commit adultery,' also said, 'Do not murder.' Now if you do not commit adultery, but you do murder, you have become a transgressor of the law" (James 2:11).

If you break one of the Ten Commandments, in fact you become a law breaker. If you break one of the Ten Commandments, you have broken all of them. When you break the law, you come under a curse. "Cursed is everyone who does not continue to do everything written in the Book of the Law."

The curse that one comes under if he breaks the Law is described in much detail in the Torah. Here is just a small part of the curse:

> "But it shall come to pass, if you do not obey the voice of the LORD your God, to observe carefully all His commandments and His statutes which I command you today, that all these curses will come upon you and overtake you:
>
> Cursed shall you be in the city and cursed shall you be in the country.
> Cursed shall be your basket and your kneading bowl.
> Cursed shall be the fruit of your body and the produce of your land, the increase of your cattle and the offspring of your flocks.
> Cursed shall you be when you come in, and cursed shall you be when you go out" (Deuteronomy 28).

THE PRICE OF BREAKING THE LAW IS DEATH

The second terrible thing that one needs to know about the Law of Moses is the terrible price of breaking this law. The price of breaking the Law of Moses is death. The Law exposed the sin of humankind, as humans failed to keep the Law. The Law did not change the price of sin. The price of sin was set in the Garden of Eden. God spoke to Adam and said to him, "Of every tree of the garden you may freely eat; but of the tree of the knowledge of good and evil you shall not eat, for in the day that you eat of it you shall surely die."

The price of sin is death. When Adam and Eve sinned in the Garden of Eden, the price of their sin was death. When a man breaks the Law of

Moses, the price of his sin is death. **"For the wages of sin is death, but the gift of God is eternal life in Christ our Lord" (Romans 6:23).**

Sin can never be paid for by performing good deeds. It doesn't matter how many times a Christian goes to the church to pray. It doesn't matter how many times a Muslim goes to the mosque. It doesn't matter if a person goes on pilgrimage. It does not matter whether or not a person performs his prayers perfectly. It does not matter if a person gives alms to the poor. All these good deeds will never pay the price of sin. The price of sin is not a good deed. The price of sin is death.

The soul who sins shall die (Ezekiel 18:20).

The Torah teaches us that just one sin ruined everything. Adam and Eve sinned by eating the forbidden fruit, and the door was opened for death to enter creation. Death spread quickly through all of creation. Soon, Adam's children were murdering each other.

During the time of Moses, the Israelites offered up animal sacrifices to pay the price for their sin. They offered up goats and sheep. When these animals were slaughtered, the death of these animals covered their sin in some small way. The price of sin is death.

Of course, there were many sins that could not be paid for with the blood of a goat or a sheep. Under the Law of Moses, if a person committed adultery, that person was stoned to death. The blood of an animal could not save him/her. Likewise, if a person broke the Sabbath, or blasphemed, or worshiped idols, or cursed his parents, or murdered someone, the blood of an animal could not save him.

Under the Law of Moses, God only accepted the blood of an animal to pay the price of some sins, mainly the unintentional sins. Even then, the blood of a single sheep did not last long. There needed to be regular, daily sacrifices to cover the sin of the Israelites.

In fact, the blood of sheep, goats, and cattle never paid the full price of any man's sin. The death of a lamb just covered that sin to some degree, so that God's anger was not immediately released. God allowed these sacrifices, so that the people of Israel would know that the wages of sin is death. As they laid their hands on a lamb, they "transferred" their sin to that lamb. As the throat of that lamb was cut by the priest, and the blood of that lamb spurted out onto the sinner, that sinner knew that the lamb was dying for his sin. He knew that the price of his sin was death.

THE BLOOD OF ANIMALS CANNOT PAY THE FULL PRICE OF SIN

As time passed, God made it clear that He was not satisfied with the sacrifices of sheep and goats. The full price for sin needed to be paid, and men's hearts needed to change.

The prophet Isaiah wrote the following message from God:

"To what purpose is the multitude of your sacrifices to Me?" Says the LORD. "I have had enough of burnt offerings of rams and the fat of fed cattle. I do not delight in the blood of bulls, Or of lambs or goats" (Isaiah 1:11).

King David is recognized as both a king and a prophet by Jews, Christians and Muslims. King David wrote the following words, as he realized that the blood of animals was not actually pleasing the Lord.

"You do not delight in sacrifice, or I would bring it; You do not take pleasure in burnt offerings. My sacrifice, O God, is a broken spirit; a broken and contrite heart you, God, will not despise" (Psalm 51:16-17).

The Law of Moses exposes sin, but it does not really offer a solution for sin. How can a sinful man walk with a holy God, when the price of sin is death? How can a mere man enter Paradise and live forever, when his sin condemns him to death? The law condemns every man because it exposes the sinful deeds of every man.

The real answer to sin is not found in the Law. The answer to sin is found in a perfect sacrifice, a sacrifice that completely pays the price of sin once and for all. God loves us, and He provides His people with a way to escape the power of sin, so that they can enter Paradise and live with Him forever. We will discuss the perfect sacrifice and the path of life that God provides for His people in the final chapter of this book.

Now let us examine each one of the Ten Commandments that were given to Moses. If we understand these Ten Commandments, we will better understand the righteousness of God and the nature of sin. If we understand these Ten Commandments, we will gain a deeper understanding of the prophet Mohammed and true Islam.

3 The First Commandment

God gave the first of the Ten Commandments to Moses with these words: "I am the LORD your God, who brought you out of the land of Egypt, out of the house of bondage. You shall have no other gods before Me" (Exodus 20:2).

Under the law of Moses, the penalty for worshiping a god other than the true God was death. Moses taught the people "If there arises among you a prophet and he performs a miracle and uses that miracle to mislead the people so that they worship and serve false gods, you should not listen to the words of that prophet. God is testing you to see whether or not you love him with all your heart and all your soul. That prophet shall be put to death, because he has tried to turn you away from God who brought you out of slavery in Egypt" (Deuteronomy 13:1-5, paraphrased),

Moses taught that if your brother or your son or your daughter or your wife or your best friend tells you to go and serve other gods instead of God, that person should not be listened to, but must be stoned to death. Even if you were very close to that person, your hand should be the first one to pick up a stone to kill him. (Deuteronomy 13:6-10)

This commandment of having no gods before God is related to another commandment found in the law of Moses: "Hear, O Israel, the LORD our God, the LORD is one. And you shall love the LORD your God with all your heart, with all your soul, with all your mind, and with all your strength" (Deuteronomy 6:4-5).

JESUS TEACHES THE FIRST COMMANDMENT

To fully understand this commandment, we must not only study the teachings of Moses. We must also study the teachings of Jesus (Isa). Jesus taught the Law of Moses to his followers hundreds of years after the death of Moses. When Jesus taught the Law of Moses, he taught it in a different way than Moses taught it. Jesus taught the law of Moses in such a way that the righteous requirements of the law penetrated the hearts of his hearers. He taught his followers that it was not enough to obey the external requirements of the Law. Even if you do what the law says, but sin is in your heart, you are a lawbreaker condemned to judgment.

Jesus taught that sin comes from the heart, not from the mind. When a man murders someone, that sin comes from the hatred that is in his heart. When a man commits adultery, that adultery comes from the sinful lust that is in that man's heart. When a man worships idols, that idol worship comes because that man does not truly love God in his heart. Jesus taught us that if a man hopes to keep the Law of Moses, his heart needs to change.

An expert in the Law of Moses came to Jesus and asked him which commandment in the Law of Moses was the greatest commandment. Jesus gave the man an unexpected answer. Instead of telling the man which one of the Ten Commandments was the most important, Jesus quoted from a different part of the Law of Moses. Jesus answered:

"The first of all the commandments is: Hear, O Israel, the LORD our God, the LORD is one. And you shall love the LORD your God with all your heart, with all your soul, with all your mind, and with all your strength.' This is the first commandment.

And the second, like it, is this: 'You shall love your neighbor as yourself.' There is no other commandment greater than these" (Mark 12:29-31).

This commandment was a part of the Law of Moses, just as the Ten Commandments were a part of the Law of Moses. The Ten Commandments told people mainly what they should not do. Jesus quoted the part of the law that told them what they should do. They should love the Lord their God with everything in them. They should love their neighbor as themselves.

In other words, the most important thing in keeping the Law of Moses was not trying hard not to do bad things. The most important thing is to have a changed heart, to be filled with the love of God. If your heart is full of love for God, everything else will follow.

If you love the Lord your God with all your heart, all your soul, and all your mind, you will automatically keep the first three commandments found in the Law of Moses. If you love God with all your heart, you will never put a false god in front of the true God. You will worship God and God alone. If you love God with all your heart, you will never worship idols. If you love God with all your heart, you will never blaspheme God or take his name in vain.

When Jesus was praying and fasting in the wilderness for 40 days, the devil came to him to tempt him. The devil took Him to a very high mountain and showed Him all the kingdoms of the world and their glory. The devil said to Jesus, "All these kingdoms I will give to you, if you will fall down and worship me. Jesus said to the devil, "Be gone, Satan! For it is written, "You shall worship the Lord your God and Him only you shall serve!" (Matthew 4:8-10).

Jesus kept the first commandment. He did not bow down to Satan, and the devil departed from Him. Jesus loved God with all His heart, soul, mind and strength, and nothing could separate Him from the One He loved.

4 The Second Commandment

"You shall not make for yourself a carved image—any likeness of anything that is in heaven above, or that is in the earth beneath, or that is in the water under the earth; you shall not bow down to them nor serve them. For I, the LORD your God, am a jealous God, visiting the iniquity of the fathers upon the children to the third and fourth generations of those who hate Me, but showing mercy to thousands, to those who love Me and keep My commandments" (Exodus 20:4-6).

The second commandment found in the Torah is, "You shall not make for yourself an idol." The Torah condemns the worship of idols more than any other sin. God hates idolatry. Men who worship idols form blood covenants with the evil spirits that are represented by those idols. These evil spirits are in rebellion against God, and those who form covenants with them join them in their rebellion.

Satan is very skilled at causing people to worship idols and evil spirits instead of the true God. Some people worship spirits and idols because of fear. They believe that if they do not worship those spirits, those spirits will cause harm to them or their family. Other people worship idols because they believe that the idols will help them to prosper and succeed in life. They believe that the spirits represented by the idol will cause their crops to grow and their businesses to flourish.

Of course, any man who worships an idol comes into an evil agreement with Satan. The devil comes to kill, to steal and to destroy. He might heal one disease in a man's body, but he will cause five more. He might heal a man's cold, but he will give that man cancer. Anyone who enters into an agreement with the devil is sure to lose.

Idol worship always involves blood sacrifice. When men worship idols, they make sacrifices to those idols. They make blood sacrifices to those idols. As they make that blood sacrifice, they are making a blood covenant with the idol and with the evil spirit that is represented by that idol. They are declaring that they belong to that idol, that everything they have belongs to that idol.

It is impossible to worship God and also to worship idols. The one who worships an idol is making an evil agreement between himself and an evil spirit. He is declaring that he belongs to that evil spirit, and not to God. He is declaring that he puts his trust in that evil spirit instead of putting his trust in God. He is connecting himself by blood covenant to those spirits that hate God and have rebelled against God.

This is why the Torah speaks of God's jealousy when it speaks of idolatry. It is impossible to have a blood covenant with a Holy God, while you have formed a blood covenant with an idol and with the evil spirit represented by that idol. When you worship an idol and form a covenant with that idol, you are breaking your covenant with God.

A woman who sleeps with a man who is not her husband breaks her covenant with her husband and arouses his anger and jealousy. In the same way, when people who are connected to God in covenant decide to worship idols and form covenants with the evil spirits who are connected to those idols, they will always stir up the anger and jealousy of God.

God loves his people with a greater love that we can even imagine. The Torah makes it very clear that the love of God is a jealous kind of love. He does not want to share His people with false gods and idols!

Take heed to yourselves, lest you forget the covenant of the LORD your God which He made with you, and make for yourselves a carved image in the form of anything which the LORD your God has forbidden you.

For the LORD your God is a consuming fire, a jealous God (Deuteronomy 4:23-24).

The penalty for idolatry is death. Moses spent 40 days on Mount Sinai, receiving the Law from God, while the Israelites waited for him to return in the desert below. As the days grew long, the Israelites became tired of waiting for Moses to return. Finally, they said to Aaron, "Come, make us gods that shall go before us; As for Moses, the man who brought us up out of the land of Egypt, we do not know what has become of him."

Aaron decided to do what the people wanted him to do. He told the people to bring all the golden earrings that were in the ears of the people. After receiving the earrings, he melted them in the fire and formed a golden idol that looked like a calf. The people said to each other, "This is your god, O Israel, that brought you out of the land of Egypt!"

The people began to sacrifice animals to this idol and to hold feasts as they ate the sacrifices. As they did so, they formed blood covenants with this idol and the evil spirits it represented. As they made these sacrifices, they declared that they belonged to this idol instead of to God.

As the people formed these covenants, they stirred up the anger of God. Moses came down from the mountain with the law that God had given him written in two tablets of stone. As he approached the camp of the Israelites, he heard the sounds of singing and celebration. The Israelites were holding a feast as they worshiped their idol, the golden calf.

When he realized what was happening, he became enraged. He smashed the tablets of stone on the ground. He burned the golden calf with fire, ground it into powder, scattered the powder on the water, and made the Israelites drink the water. He confronted his brother Aaron who made the idol and helped the Israelites in their sin. Then he called out, "Whoever is on God's side, come to me!" The tribe of Levi gathered together behind Moses.

Moses said to them, "Thus says the Lord God of Israel: Let every man put his sword on his side and go throughout the camp, and let every man kill his brother, his companion and his neighbor."

And so, the Levites obeyed the words of Moses. They went through the camp of the Israelites, killing those people who worshiped idols. They killed about 3,000 men that day. The price of idolatry is death.

5 The Third Commandment

The third commandment of the Ten Commandments is written this way:

"You shall not take the name of the LORD your God in vain, for the LORD will not hold him guiltless who takes His name in vain" (Exodus 20:7).

What does it mean to take the Lord's name in vain? There are two ways that a man can take the Lord's name in vain. In the first case, a man who curses the name of the Lord, or blasphemes against God, has taken the Lord's name in vain. Under the Law of Moses, the penalty for cursing God in this way was death.

On one occasion, the son of an Israelite woman and an Egyptian father got into a fight with an Israelite. During the fight, this man cursed and blasphemed the name of the Lord. The people heard what he had done, and they brought him to Moses. The Lord spoke to Moses and told him, "Take this man who has cursed God outside the camp. Let everyone who heard him curse put their hands on his head, and then let the people stone him" (Leviticus 24:10-15). And so it was done.

Moses continued to teach the word of the Lord: "Whoever blasphemes the name of the Lord shall surely be put to death. All the congregation shall certainly stone him, the stranger as well as him who is born in the land. When he blasphemes the name of the Lord, he shall be put to death" (Leviticus 24:16).

USING THE NAME OF GOD WRONGLY

There is a second way that a man can take the Lord's name in vain. If a man uses the Lord's name wrongly, he has taken that name in vain. If someone speaks in the name of God, and says that it will not rain for 40 days, and after five days it begins raining, that person has spoken wrongly in the name of God. The price for speaking wrongly in the name of God is death.

Moses spoke the word of God, "The prophet who presumes to speak a word in my name, which I have not commanded him to speak, or who speaks in the name of other gods, that prophet shall die."

The people asked Moses "How shall we know whether or not God has spoken through a prophet?"

Moses answered "When a prophet speaks in the name of the Lord, if the thing that he spoke about does not happen or come to pass, then the Lord has not spoke. The prophet has spoken presumptuously, and you should not be afraid of him."

Under the Law of Moses, it was a very dangerous thing to speak in the name of God. If you add to God's words, you will be found guilty. If you take away from his words, you will be found guilty.

It is wrong to use the name of the Lord foolishly. There came a time when Moses spoke in the name of God. The Israelites were marching through the desert, and they ran out of water. They began to complain bitterly against their leader, Moses. Moses became very frustrated with the people.

Moses went to the tabernacle where he met with God, and fell on his face. The Lord spoke to Moses and told him to take his rod and to go and speak to a rock, and that water would flow from the rock for the Israelites and their animals.

And so, Moses went out to the rock with his rod, as all the Israelites watched. With great anger, he yelled at the Israelites, "Here now, you rebels! Must we bring water for you out of this rock?" Then, instead of speaking to the rock, he angrily struck the rock twice with his staff (Numbers 20:2-12).

As he struck the rock, and spoke with great anger to the people, he did so in the name of God. He made it clear that God was very angry.

In fact, it was Moses who was very angry, not God. As Moses acted in anger, and spoke in the name of God, saying, "Must We (Moses and God) bring you water from out of this rock?", he was actually speaking wrongly in the name of God. He was pretending that his anger was God's anger. As he beat the rock with his staff, he was actually disobeying God, who told Moses to only "speak" to the rock.

Water came from the rock as Moses struck it, but Moses had spoken wrongly in the name of God. Therefore, God told Moses that he would not be allowed to lead the Israelites out of the desert and into the Promised Land, the land of Abraham.

It is dangerous to speak in the name of God and to condemn someone in His name. It is dangerous to say, "God damn you" or to condemn anyone. What if you are wrong? What if you have spoken God's judgment over someone in a wrong way? What if you didn't see very clearly, and you condemned someone who God has not condemned? Will you be held guiltless?

SINNING IN THE NAME OF THE LORD

Men have committed terrible sins while using the name of God to justify their actions. Some men commit murder and rape and claim that God is the one leading them to do these things. Some men steal from others and claim that God is the one leading them to steal. Some men tell lies and claim that God is the one who allows them to lie. Every man who commits sin and claims that God is the one causing him to sin is guilty of blasphemy and using the Lord's name in vain. Every man who does these things will be found guilty on the Day of Judgment.

JESUS TEACHES THE THIRD COMMANDMENT

Jesus warned his listeners not to use the Lord's name in vain. He taught people not to swear using the name of God. He taught them to speak simple words, without trying to add power to their words by speaking them in the name of God. He taught people not to swear by God's heaven, or by God's earth, but simply to speak the truth in every circumstance. He taught, "Let your 'Yes' be 'Yes' and your 'No' be 'No.'" He taught that if you try to add to the power of your words by swearing by God or his creation, you are actually being motivated by Satan.

Here is the teaching from the Injil:

"Again you have heard that it was said to those of old, 'You shall not swear falsely, but shall perform your oaths to the Lord.' But I say to you, do not swear at all: neither by heaven, for it is God's throne; nor by the earth, for it is His footstool; nor by Jerusalem, for it is the city of the great King. Nor shall you swear by your head, because you cannot make one hair white or black. But let your 'Yes' be 'Yes,' and your 'No,' 'No.' For whatever is more than these is from the evil one" (Matthew 5:33-37).

6 The Fourth Commandment

The Law of Moses contains a commandment that very few people follow today, whether Christian, or Muslim, or Jew. The fourth commandment is stated this way:

> **Remember the Sabbath day, to keep it holy. Six days you shall labor and do all your work, but the seventh day is the Sabbath of the Lord your God. In it you shall do no work: you, nor your son, nor your daughter, nor your male servant, nor your female servant, nor your stranger who is within your gates. For in six days the Lord made the heavens and the earth, the sea, and all that is in them, and rested the seventh day. Therefore the Lord blessed the Sabbath day and hallowed it (Exodus 20:8-11).**

Most Christians do not keep the Sabbath day today. Some Christians refuse to work on Sunday, but Sunday was not the seventh day of the week. Saturday is the Sabbath, the seventh day of the week. Likewise, most Jews do not keep the Sabbath in the way that Moses taught them to keep it.

Under the Law of Moses, the price for breaking the Sabbath was very severe. Under the Law of Moses, the price of breaking the Sabbath was death. Moses declared the word of the Lord: "You shall keep the Sabbath, therefore, for it is holy to you. Everyone who profanes it shall surely be put to death....Work shall be done for six days but the seventh is the Sabbath of rest, holy to the Lord. Whoever does any work on the Sabbath day, he shall surely be put to death" (Exodus 31:14-15).

While the Israelites were in the desert, they found a man gathering firewood on the Sabbath. They brought the man to Moses and Aaron. The Lord said to Moses, "The man must surely be put to death. All the congregation shall stone him with stones outside the camp." And so the man was taken outside the camp and stoned (Numbers 15:32-36).

JESUS AND THE SABBATH

Jesus taught about the Sabbath in a different way. When Jesus taught the Sabbath, he emphasized the fact that the Sabbath was made by God as a gift for man. Sabbath was given by God to man as a day of rest. It was a day in which God would bless the rest of man. Even though a man did no work on that day, God would supernaturally bless his business so much during the other six days that he would not lose anything by resting on the seventh day. In other words, the Sabbath was a day when man could rest, and God would work for him. It was a day of blessing that even as man rested God would take care of his crops and his business.

For Jesus, the Sabbath was a day of miracles. Jesus loved to heal people and perform miracles on the Sabbath. These miracles were not the result of a man's sweat and hard work. They were the supernatural work of God.

During the days of Jesus, there were many experts in the Law of Moses known as Pharisees. These Pharisees wanted to condemn Jesus because they hated his preaching. They hated the way Jesus confronted the hearts of people, exposing their hidden sin. The Pharisees were experts on changing the outside of a person. They knew how to dress in a way that seemed very religious and correct, in a way that impressed people. They knew how to pray in a way that seemed very religious and correct, in a way that impressed people. In spite of their religious activities, their hearts were far from God.

One Sabbath day, Jesus was in the house of one of the Pharisees, eating bread with him on the Sabbath. The Pharisees were watching Jesus closely. They hoped that he would break the Law of Moses so that they could accuse him and condemn him.

A man with dropsy was brought to Jesus. Before Jesus healed the man, He asked the Pharisees a question, "Is it lawful to heal on the Sabbath?" The Pharisees were afraid to answer Him, and they kept silent. Jesus then took the man and healed him, and sent him away. Then he rebuked the Pharisees saying, "Which of you, having a donkey or an ox that has fallen into a pit, will not immediately pull him out on the Sabbath day?"

The Pharisees were unable to answer him anything (Luke 14:1-11).

On another Sabbath day, Jesus was teaching the word of God in a Jewish synagogue. There was a woman in the gathering who had been crippled for 18 years. She was bent over and could not raise herself up in any way. When Jesus saw her, He said to her, "Woman, you are freed from your infirmity!" He laid his hands on her, and immediately she was healed. She stood up straight and glorified God.

The leader of the synagogue became angry and said to the people "There are six days on which men ought to work. Therefore come and be healed on those six days, and not on the Sabbath day."

Jesus rebuked the man and said to him, "Hypocrite! Does not each one of you on the Sabbath release his ox or donkey from the stall and lead it to water? Shouldn't this woman, a daughter of Abraham, whom Satan has bound for eighteen years, be set free from this bondage on the Sabbath?" (Luke 13:10-16).

On another Sabbath, Jesus was involved in a confrontation with the Pharisees in the temple in Jerusalem. When Jesus left the temple, He met a blind man begging for money. The man had been blind from the day he was born.

Jesus spit on the ground and made mud with the saliva and dirt. He took the mud and rubbed it on the man's eyes. He told the man, "Go and wash in the pool of Siloam." The man went and washed his eyes in the pool. When he did so, he began to see for the first time in his life.

Those who knew the man began to ask one another, "Isn't that the blind man who used to beg for money?" Some thought it was the man, while others thought he only resembled the man. The man himself said, "I am he!" He told them what Jesus had done for him.

The Pharisees began to argue with the miracle. They claimed that Jesus had broken the Sabbath when He healed on the Sabbath. They declared that God would never use a Sabbath-breaker to do His work. They did not believe the man's story. They began to question the man's parents. The parents confirmed that the man was born blind and that a miracle had taken place.

Finally, the Pharisees questioned the man himself. They said, "Give God the glory for your healing. We know that Jesus is only a sinner!"

The man answered them, "Whether He is a sinner or not I do not know. One thing I know--that though I was blind, now I see."

The Pharisees continued to argue with him, and to accuse Jesus. They knew the details of the Law of Moses, but they did not understand the heart of God. A great miracle had taken place right in front of them, but they could not see what had happened. Jesus said to the Pharisees, "For judgment I have come into this world, that those who do not see may see, and that those who see may be made blind."

The Pharisees asked him, "Are you saying we are blind?"

Jesus said to them, "If you were blind, you would have no sin; but because you say, 'We see,' your sin remains" (John 9).

What can we learn from these stories? The Sabbath is a day that people should know that no matter how hard they work, there are some things that only God can do. Only God can perform miracles. Only God can open the eyes of a blind man. Only God can save us from our sins. No matter how hard we work, no matter how much we pray, we cannot pay the price of sin. Only God can save us from death and the judgment of hell.

The Sabbath is a day that a man can rest from his labor and focus on the things that only God can do. It is a day of giving thanks.

The Sabbath is a gift from God. Jesus said, "The Sabbath was made for man, and not man for the Sabbath!" (Mark 2:27).

7 The Fifth commandment

"Honor your father and your mother, that your days may be long upon the land which the LORD your God is giving you." (Exodus 20:12)

The fifth commandment of Moses was a commandment with a promise: Honor your father and mother, so that your days may be long upon the land which the Lord your God is giving you. This promise was made to the children of Abraham, that if they honor their parents, God will watch over them to that they may live long in the land.

"And he who strikes his father or his mother shall surely be put to death" (Exodus 21:15).

"And he who curses his father or his mother shall surely be put to death" (Exodus 21:17).

Under the Law of Moses, the penalty for breaking the fifth commandment was death. Under the Law of Moses, the penalty for cursing one's parents was death. The penalty for striking one's father or mother was death. Moses taught the children of Israel, "If someone has a stubborn and rebellious son who does not obey his father and mother and will not listen to them when they discipline him, his father and mother shall take hold of him and bring him to the elders at the gate of his town. They shall say to the elders, 'This son of ours is stubborn and rebellious. He will not obey us. He is a glutton and a drunkard. Then all the men of his town are to stone him to death. You must purge the evil from among you. All Israel will hear of it and be afraid'" (Deuteronomy 21:18-21).

JESUS AND THE FIFTH COMMANDMENT

Jesus taught about this commandment. During the days of Jesus, there were some very religious men who decided that they should honor God instead of their parents. So, they went to their parents, and said to them: "The honor I would have given to you, I am giving to God instead." From that moment on, they didn't do anything for their parents.

Jesus rebuked these religious men. He said, "Isaiah prophesied about you hypocrites, when he wrote these words:

"This people honors me with their lips, but their heart is far from me; in vain do they worship me, teaching as doctrines the commandments of men.' You leave the commandment of God and hold to the tradition of men."

"You have a fine way of rejecting the commandment of God in order to establish your tradition!" (Matthew 7:6-9).

Jesus made it clear that these men were disobeying the commandment of God when they dishonored their parents. It did not matter if they claimed to be honoring God when they dishonored their parents. What mattered was the fact that they had disobeyed the commandment of God. How can you honor God when you disobey His commandments?

Once again, Jesus exposed the hypocrisy of religious men. Religious men do things that look good on the outside. They dress in religious ways and they seem very dedicated to the commands of God. But their hearts are far from God. They do not actually know God or walk closely with Him. They might obey a book of rules and commands, but they do not actually know the one who gave those commands. Because of this, they always miss the mark.

Jesus taught that the religious experts of His day were not on the road leading to heaven. They were trying hard to keep the law, but their hearts were far from God. Jesus said to his followers, "I say to you, that unless your righteousness exceeds the righteousness of the scribes and Pharisees, you will by no means enter the kingdom of heaven." (Matthew 5:20)

Jesus spoke about these religious men:

"Woe to you, teachers of the law and Pharisees, you hypocrites! You clean the outside of the cup and dish, but inside they are full of greed and self-indulgence. Blind Pharisee! First clean the inside of the cup and dish, and then the outside also will be clean."

"Woe to you, teachers of the law and Pharisees, you hypocrites! You are like whitewashed tombs, which look beautiful on the outside but on the inside are full of the bones of the dead and everything unclean. In the same way, on the outside you appear to people as righteous, but on the inside you are full of hypocrisy and wickedness...

"You snakes! You brood of vipers! How will you escape being condemned to hell?" (Matthew 23).

Jesus made it clear that the condemnation of religious men who seem righteous on the outside, but have hearts full of greed will be greater than the condemnation of prostitutes and criminals. These religious men know how to impress men with their religious talk and actions, but their hearts selfishly seek their own desires. Everything they do is for the praise of men. Everything they do is for selfish reasons. Their hearts are far from God. They do not love God, and they do not love men.

"Woe to you, scribes and Pharisees, hypocrites, because you devour widows' houses, and for a pretense you make long prayers; therefore you will receive greater condemnation."

These religious men make long prayers to impress the people who are listening. They cheat people, even widows. On the Day of Judgment, they will receive the greatest condemnation.

8 The Sixth Commandment

You shall not murder (Exodus 20:13).

The sixth commandment taught by Moses is "You shall not murder." Under the Law of Moses, the penalty for murder was death. It is written in the Law, "He who strikes a man so that he dies shall surely be put to death (Exodus 21:12). It is written in the Law, "Whoever kills any man shall surely be put to death" (Leviticus 24:17). It is written in the Law, "Whoever kills an animal shall restore it, but whoever kills a man shall be put to death" (Leviticus 24:21).

Under the Law of Moses, a man could not be convicted of murder based on the testimony of a single witness. There needed to be at least two or three witnesses to convict a murderer and put him to death. It is written, "Whoever kills a person, the murderer shall be put to death on the testimony of witnesses; but one witness is not sufficient testimony against a person for the death penalty" (Numbers 35:30).

Under the Law of Moses, when murder was committed, there was no such thing as a "blood price." A murderer and his family could not pay money to the family of the one who was murdered in order to escape the punishment of death. It is written in the Law, "You shall take no ransom for the life of a murderer who is guilty of death, but he shall surely be put to death" (Numbers 35:31).

The price of murder is death. This sin cannot be paid for with blood money or any other kind of payment.

JESUS AND THE SIXTH COMMANDMENT

When Jesus taught the Ten Commandments, he taught them in such a way that the Law of Moses pierced the hearts of people. It was not enough to keep the commandments only with one's actions. If a person hoped to keep the commandments, sin needed to be removed from that person's heart.

Jesus taught, "You have heard that it was said to those of old, 'You shall not murder, and whoever murders will be in danger of the judgment.' But I say to you that whoever is angry with his brother without a cause shall be in danger of the judgment. And whoever says to his brother, 'Raca!' shall be in danger of the council. But whoever says, 'You fool!' shall be in danger of hell fire" (Matthew 5:21-22).

Jesus was teaching about this commandment, the one that says, "You shall not murder." Jesus taught that the cause of murder is the anger and hatred that is hidden in a man's heart. The man who despises his brother in this way is guilty. The anger and hatred that he hides in his heart is a sin equivalent to murder in God's eyes.

God is holy. The things that are acceptable to man are not acceptable to God! When a man is full of rage and bitterness towards someone, he may think that his rage is completely justified, that he has every right to despise his brother. He may think that as long as he did not commit murder, his anger is not a sin.

When that man comes before the throne of God, his rage and bitterness will be exposed. It does not come from God. It comes from the evil one. If that man does not know the perfect sacrifice for sin, he will be destroyed. God will never allow the hatred, rage, and bitterness of the devil to enter heaven.

When you stand before the judgment seat of God, you will not only be judged for the actions that you took. You will also be judged for what was in your heart. If you hated your brother, you will be as guilty before God as if you had actually killed your brother.

Moses taught us not to murder. Jesus taught us that if our hearts are full of anger and hatred towards our brother, we will be judged just like a murderer is judged.

THE LAWS OF WAR

When we speak of murder, the question will always come, "Does God really command his people to go to war in his name?" In the Torah, we read that Moses was instructed by God to destroy the Amorites. In the Quran we read about jihad. When is killing justified? When are men permitted to bring God's judgment upon other men?

There is a principal found in the Torah and in the Injil. Jesus said, "In the same way that you judge others, you will be judged." If God uses you to bring His judgments, you must be perfect. Otherwise, even though God may use you to judge others, He will also judge you.

In the case of Moses, God instructed him to destroy the Amorite nations. If we carefully read the Torah, we can understand the reasons why it was necessary for these nations to be destroyed. If we look at the whole story, we will also understand how dangerous it is to be used by God to bring judgment upon others. In the same way that you judge others, you will be judged. Israel brought God's judgment upon the Amorites, but when Israel sinned, the same judgments came upon them.

In Deuteronomy 20 of the Torah, the nation of Israel is instructed about warfare. When an enemy surrenders, and opens its gates, the people were not to be harmed, but could be subjected to forced labor. When an enemy resisted and a siege was required, they were to be dealt with more severely. However, certain nations were to be completely destroyed without mercy. The Amorites and the related nations that lived in the land of Canaan were to be completely destroyed, down to the last person.

However, in the cities of the nations the Lord your God is giving you as an inheritance, do not leave alive anything that

breathes. Completely destroy them—the Hittites, Amorites, Canaanites, Perizzites, Hivites and Jebusites—as the Lord your God has commanded you. Otherwise, they will teach you to follow all the detestable things they do in worshiping their gods, and you will sin against the Lord your God (Deuteronomy 20:16-18).

Why would God do this? Why would the same God who ordered Moses, "Do not murder" order the Israelites to destroy every single Amorite?

The Amorites were a people whose rebellion against God had reached such a degree that it was time for them to be destroyed. Sin is like a cancer that spreads throughout a person's body. If the cancerous growths are allowed to live and continue, they will eventually kill the man. In the same way, when a nation completely embraces evil and turns away from all knowledge of the living God, it is better for that nation to be completely destroyed, than for that nation to be allowed to continue spreading its cancer throughout the earth.

This was the situation with the Amorite nation. The Amorites were not ordinary idol worshipers. The Amorites were involved in the worship of idols and false gods to such a degree that they would sacrifice their own children to their false gods. They called this "passing their sons through the fire." The Amorites worshiped the false god Molech.

The Amorites were known for extreme sexual immorality. Moses wrote about this immorality in Leviticus 18 and in other places. As they worshiped evil spiritual beings, those evil beings encouraged the Amorites to participate in every kind of perverse sexual ritual. Men defiled themselves by having sexual relations with other men. Women defiled themselves by sleeping with women. Men and women had sexual relations with animals.

When the Amorites worshiped their idols, they would form blood covenants with the evil spirits that were represented by those idols. These blood covenants were formed in different ways. Sometimes a sheep or goat would be sacrificed to that idol, and the idol worshipers would then hold a feast in which everyone would eat the meat of that goat. As they ate the meat of the goat, they formed a blood covenant with the evil spirits that were represented by that idol. In a blood covenant, two become one. As they ate the meat of that goat, the people gave themselves to the evil spirits. They gave themselves to Molech, the evil "god" of the Amorites.

The temples of Molech also had temple prostitutes. When men worshiped Molech, they went to the temple and slept with the prostitute of the temple. As they did so, they formed a blood covenant with the evil spirit Molech, who was represented by those prostitutes.

God knew that if the Amorites were not destroyed, they would soon spread their sin and perversion to the Israelites. God knew that if the Amorites were not destroyed, they would invite the Israelites to their feasts. The Israelites would eat the meat that had been sacrificed to Molech, and they would enter a blood covenant with Molech. They would become the people of Molech. The Israelites would become bound by blood covenants with false idols. They would eventually become just as evil as the Amorites had become.

GOD'S WARNINGS TO THE AMORITES

God never destroys a nation without first sending his messengers to warn that nation. In the case of the Amorites, the messengers of God spoke the word of God in that region for many generations. Long before the days of Moses, Abraham lived among the Amorites and testified of the living God. The great high priest of God, Melchizedek, also lived and testified among the Amorites in the land of Canaan. In those days there were two cities that existed in that region, Sodom and Gomorrah. These two cities were extremely evil--so evil that God was about to destroy them by fire. Extreme sexual perversion became normal in these cities.

God told Abraham that if he could find even ten righteous men in Sodom, He would spare the city. Unfortunately, ten righteous men were not found and the time of destruction came upon the city.

Abraham's nephew, Lot, lived in Sodom. God sent two angels to warn Lot to flee from Sodom. The people of Sodom were so perverse that all the men of the city gathered together to try to attack and rape the angels. The angels took refuge in Lot's house, as God struck the men of the city blind. The next day, Lot and his family fled the city. The city was destroyed by fire falling from heaven.

The Amorites did not repent even though they saw Sodom and Gomorrah destroyed by the fire of God. When the Israelites were delivered from Egypt with many miracles and marched towards the Promised Land, it took 40 years for the Israelites to arrive in the land of the Amorites. For 40 years the Amorites heard the stories of Israel's deliverance from Egypt. For 40 years they heard the stories of the living God. They heard the stories of the supernatural plagues that came upon the Egyptians because they refused to repent. They heard the story of the parting of the Red Sea, the deliverance of Israel, and the destruction of Pharaoh's army. For 40 years they told these stories to one another, but they did not repent of their sin and idolatry. They loved their sin, they hated God, and they were destroyed.

WHOM DID GOD USE TO JUDGE THE AMORITES?

The Amorites certainly deserved the judgment of God. They deserved to be destroyed. But who can God use to bring this judgment? The one who brings God's judgment must be free of sin. Otherwise, after he brings God's judgment upon evildoers because of their sin, he must also face the judgment of God for his own sin.

It is very dangerous to be used by God to bring judgment. This is why the Israelites spent years wandering in the wilderness before God allowed them to enter into the land of Canaan. God could not allow the nation of Israel to bring His judgment against the Amorites until the nation of Israel was cleansed from its own sin. The nation of Israel needed to learn the ways of God. They needed to receive His Law and to follow it with all of their heart. Only then could they bring God's judgment upon the Amorites without being destroyed themselves.

In the wilderness, the generation that God delivered from slavery in Egypt hardened their hearts and failed the tests. They began to complain and criticize. They complained about the food that they ate, the manna that came from heaven every day. They complained against God who had delivered them out of slavery. They complained about the leadership of Moses, whom God used to deliver them. Finally, when it came time for them to enter the land of Canaan and fight the Amorites, they became afraid and started accusing Moses of wanting to kill them. They demanded that he return them to Egypt.

And so God judged them. He told them that because of their complaining and hardness of hearts, they would wander for 40 years in the wilderness. The entire generation that God delivered from slavery in Egypt died in the desert. Their children watched them die. Moses also died without entering the promised land.

After Moses died, Joshua became the new leader of the Israelites. Joshua led a new generation of Israelites towards the promised land, towards the land of Canaan. The Israelites of this generation were the ones who watched their parents die in the desert. This new generation decided not to follow the example of their parents. They decided to obey God completely, without complaining and rebellion.

And so the generation that followed Joshua kept the Law of Moses. They obeyed God, and He led them into the land of Canaan where they defeated many Amorite armies. They took possession of the land of Canaan, which today is called Israel and Palestine.

It did not take long for sin to enter the army of the Israelites. The first battle that the Israelites fought under the command of Joshua was the battle of Jericho. The Lord instructed Joshua to have his army march around the walls of Jericho for six days, once each day. On the seventh day, the army marched seven times around the walls of Jericho. Then Joshua blew his trumpet, and the walls of Jericho fell to the ground. The Israelite army rushed into Jericho to destroy the Amorites who lived there.

Before the battle of Jericho began, Joshua instructed his army that all the silver and gold in the city was to be dedicated to the Lord. As the Israelite soldiers rushed the city, one man named Achan saw some treasure that he desired for himself. He took a beautiful Babylonian garment, two hundred shekels of silver, and a wedge of gold weighing fifty shekels. He hid this stolen treasure in his tent.

After the battle of Jericho, the Israelites faced a much smaller city, the city of Ai. After the great victory that took place at Jericho, the Israelites believed that they would easily conquer Ai. They did not even send their complete army to fight the city of Ai.

When the battle with Ai began, the men of Ai began to defeat the army of Israel. God did not give the Israelites boldness and victory as He did in the battle of Jericho. The Israelite men ran from their enemies like scared children.

Joshua was shocked. He tore his clothes, fell on the ground and cried out to God, "Oh, God, why have you brought us here? Are you going to deliver us into the hands of the Amorites?"

The Lord rebuked Joshua. "Get up! Why do you lie on your face? Israel has sinned. They have broken my covenant. They have stolen some of the things that they were not supposed to take. Therefore, they could not stand before their enemies…" (Joshua 7:12).

The Israelites drew lots to discover who had stolen from the Lord. The lot fell on Achan. Joshua asked Achan to confess what he had done. Achan confessed that he had stolen a Babylonian garment, some silver, and a wedge of gold and buried them under his tent. And so Achan and his entire family were condemned to death, and the nation of Israel stoned them to death.

When the sin and the sinners were removed from the nation, God enabled Israel to stand once again. From that moment on, none of the armies of the Amorite nations were able to stand before Israel. All of them were defeated and destroyed.

From this story, we learn that when one man named Achan sinned, judgment came upon the entire nation. Achan stole some gold and silver, and the entire army of Israel was defeated by their enemies! It is not easy to be used by God to bring judgment!

The entire nation of Israel needed to be sinless before they could be used by God to bring judgment upon the Amorites. Otherwise, after the Israelites judged the Amorites, Israel would also be judged with the same judgment.

Do not judge, or you too will be judged. For in the same way you judge others, you will be judged, and with the measure you use, it will be measured to you (Matthew 7:1-2).

In fact, there were only brief moments in Israel's history when the nation was without sin. After Israel defeated the Amorites, Israel soon began sinning. Soon idolatry and other sins filled the nation. Soon God's judgment came upon Israel, just as it had come upon the Amorites. In the end, God judged the Israelites so severely that their temple was destroyed, their capital city Jerusalem was destroyed, and the Israelites became the slaves of their enemies.

Your sins will not be forgiven because you become involved in a jihad. The one who judges others will be judged more severely by God. Going on jihad will not pay the price for your sins. In fact, you should be completely without sin before you ever become involved in jihad! Otherwise, after you have brought God's judgment upon others for their sins, you will also be judged for your own sin! This is the message of the Torah and the message of Jesus.

THE PERFECTION OF GOD

The Law of Moses provided an incredibly high standard of righteousness that seemed almost impossible for anyone to meet. When the nation of Israel was used by God to bring judgment upon the Amorites, the entire nation needed to be free of sin. If even one person broke the law, the entire nation was guilty. The entire nation suffered under the judgment of God.

This seems extreme, but God is holy. When one man named Adam sinned, the door was opened for sin to enter the entire human race. Sin has polluted the human race since that time.

When Jesus came, you might think that he would make things easier for his followers. He did not. In fact when Jesus taught the Law of Moses, he taught this Law in such a way that it seemed impossible for any man to keep the Law. Jesus raised the level of righteousness required by God much, much higher than Moses did.

The Law of Moses judges the actions of a person. Jesus was able to judge a person's heart. Jesus could look past the outside of a person and see directly into his heart. He could see when a person was motivated by greed or rebellion. It did not matter what kind of excuses the person might make for his actions, Jesus could see the real reasons that caused that person to do what he did.

In fact, Jesus taught that the level of righteousness required by God was actually perfection. When Jesus taught about the law of Moses, He summed up his teachings with the words, "Therefore you shall be perfect, just as your Father in heaven is perfect" (Matthew 5:48).

This is the real level of righteousness that God is looking for. He is not looking for a people who merely keep themselves from committing murder and adultery and other sins. He is looking for a people who have been completely transformed. He is looking for people who are perfect, as God is perfect. He is looking for a people who love the way God loves, who act the way God acts. He is looking for a people who have the character of God Himself.

Who has walked in the perfection of God? Which person is without sin? A person might be able to keep the external requirements of the Law. He might be able to keep from killing another man or committing adultery. But which person has never had bitter, unrighteous anger in his heart towards another? Which man has truly kept the law of God?

A MUCH STRICTER JUDGMENT

Not only did Jesus raise the level of righteousness that was required by God. Jesus also raised the price of sin. The cost of breaking the laws of God did not go down. It went up. Moses taught repeatedly that the price of breaking the Law was death. Jesus taught about a penalty for sin that was much, much worse than death. Jesus taught about the eternal judgment of the last day. He spoke of a lake of fire. He said that only a few would escape the condemnation of hell.

"Enter by the narrow gate; for wide is the gate and broad is the way that leads to destruction, and there are many who go in by it. Because narrow is the gate and difficult is the way which leads to life, and there are few who find it" (Matthew 7:13-14).

Jesus made it clear that the price of sin was extremely high, so high that a person should do anything in his power to keep from sinning. Jesus said, "If your hand or foot causes you to sin, cut it off and cast it from you. It is better for you to enter into life lame or maimed, rather than having two hands or two feet, to be cast into the everlasting fire. And if your eye causes you to sin, pluck it out and cast it from you. It is better for you to enter into life with one eye, rather than having two eyes, to be cast into hell fire (Matthew 18:8-9).

Jesus taught that sin is not merely what can be seen on the outside of a person. Sin includes that which is in the heart of a person, the evil desires that no one can see. These evil desires in a person's heart will lead him to hell just as surely as committing a crime. Jesus taught that the real price of sin is eternal punishment, which is also known as the "second death."

THE MERCY OF GOD

If the righteousness required by the Law is such a high level of righteousness that no ordinary person can actually walk in that righteousness, and if the penalty of sin is eternal judgment, what hope does a person have? If these things are true, what should people do?

First of all, persons must stop judging one another. If the level of righteousness required by God is so high, then no person is truly righteous. Every person is a sinner. Does a sinner have the right to judge another sinner? If you are a lawbreaker, should you be trying to judge and punish other lawbreakers? Of course not. If you are a lawbreaker, you should be busy trying to change your own life.

Therefore, Jesus taught His followers not to judge others, but to seek God's mercy and forgiveness for themselves. Jesus made it very clear that there is a road that leads to life. There is a road that leads to forgiveness of sins. It is a narrow road, a difficult road. If you desire to walk on this path of life, you must stop judging others and seek God's mercy for your own life. If you judge others, you will surely receive God's full judgment for your sins.

This is why Jesus taught His disciples not to fight with swords for His kingdom. Jesus did not tell His followers to judge the evil of this earth with their swords. Jesus taught His followers to deal with the sin that was in their own hearts, instead of using swords to try to punish the sins of others.

Jesus taught about the kingdom of heaven that was coming to earth. When that kingdom comes, an eternal judgment will also come. God will expose every hidden thing. He will expose every sinful lust that has lived in a person's heart. He will expose greed and idolatry that has hidden deep in a heart. He will punish many with eternal punishment. And some will be saved from their sins. They will put their trust in the only One who can save them. They will be completely delivered from sin, and they will live with God forever.

9 The Eighth Commandment

Let us now look at the eighth of the Ten Commandments found in the Law of Moses: "You shall not steal" (Exodus 20:15). Once again, the penalty for stealing under the Law of Moses was severe. The penalty for stealing under the Law of Moses varied according to the severity of the theft. If a man stole an ox or a sheep and it was found alive in his possession, the thief needed to pay back double what he had stolen. On the other hand, if a man stole an ox or a sheep and slaughtered it or sold it, he was expected to repay five oxen for the ox that he stole, and four sheep for the sheep that he stole (Exodus 22:3-4).

If someone kidnapped a man, and sold that man as a slave, the penalty was much higher. The penalty for this type of theft was death. "He who kidnaps a man and sells him, or if he is found in his hand, shall surely be put to death" (Exodus 22:1).

Jesus taught about stealing in a different way than Moses did. On one occasion a certain young ruler came to Jesus and asked Him, "Good Teacher, what shall I do to inherit eternal life?"

Jesus said to the man, "Why do you call me good? No one is good but One, that is, God."

This confirmed the teachings of Jesus. Jesus taught that for one to be truly righteous, he needed to be perfect, like God. Of course, Jesus knew men's hearts, and He knew that no man actually walked in the righteousness of God.

Then, Jesus asked the man if he kept the Law of Moses. He said to him, "You know the commandments: Do not commit adultery. Do not murder. Do not steal…." Jesus listed the commandments of Moses. The young man believed that he had kept these commandments. He said, "All these things I have kept from my youth."

Jesus said to him, "You still lack one thing. Sell all that you have, and distribute to the poor, and you will have treasure in heaven; and come, follow Me."

The young man turned and walked away with much sorrow, because he was very rich. And when Jesus saw the man's sorrow, He said, "How hard it is for those who have riches to enter the kingdom of heaven!"(Luke 18:18-24).

Jesus could see that the young man's heart was filled with the love of money. It might be true that this young man had never stolen from anyone, as he claimed. However, he still loved money, just like a thief loves money. He held on to his money, and he was unwilling to leave his money and follow the prophet.

Jesus saw into the man's heart. He saw that this man had an idol in his heart. His idol was money. This money meant more to him than anything else.

Jesus taught his followers that they should not love money. Jesus taught them that they should give their money away to those who asked them for help. He taught them not to hold onto money so tightly. He taught them that if were possible to use the money they had to bless someone else, they should do it.

This is the teaching of Jesus. Not only should you not steal. You should give, as God gives. God gives his sunshine to good men and evil men. The rain falls on good men and on evil men. Those who have the heart of God should do what is in their power to bless and help whomever they can.

There was another rich man who came to Jesus. His name was Zacchaeus. Zacchaeus was a thief. He worked as a tax collector for the Romans. He often forced people to pay more tax than they should have paid. He kept the extra money for himself.

When Zacchaeus heard that Jesus was preaching, he felt a burning desire inside to hear the words of Jesus. Zacchaeus was a very short man, and he was unable to see Jesus because of the crowd. Then Zacchaeus saw a sycamore tree growing on the path that Jesus was walking on. Zacchaeus climbed the tree, so that he could see Jesus when He passed by.

As Jesus walked by, he looked up into the tree and called Zacchaeus by name, "Zacchaeus, hurry up and come down, for today I must stay at your house."

Zacchaeus was overjoyed. How did Jesus know his name? This must surely be a great prophet! Zacchaeus came down out of the tree and invited Jesus into his house.

The religious men were angry. They said, "Jesus is the guest of a man who is a thief and a sinner."

Zacchaeus was surely a sinner but when Jesus visited his house, he repented of his sin. He said to Jesus, "Lord, I will give half of my goods to the poor; and if I have taken anything from anyone, I will pay it back four times over!"

Jesus said of Zacchaeus, "Today salvation has come to this house, because he also is a son of Abraham; for the Son of Man has come to seek and to save that which was lost" (Luke 10:5-10).

The rich young ruler never stole from anyone, but he loved money. He had the heart of a thief, and he walked away from Jesus with condemnation. Zacchaeus was a thief, but he had a heart that truly loved God. When he met Jesus, he paid back everything he had stolen. Zacchaeus was a true son of Abraham.

A TRANSFORMED HEART

When Jesus taught about the Law of Moses, He taught about the hearts of men. He taught that everything flows out of the heart, whether good or evil. Good men take good things out of their hearts and spread them to the world. Evil men take evil things out of their hearts and spread them into the world.

In fact, the only way to truly fulfill the Law of Moses is to have a transformed heart. A teacher of the law asked Jesus which was the greatest commandment. Jesus answered, "The first of all the commandments is: 'Hear, O Israel, the LORD our God, the LORD is one. And you shall love the LORD your God with all your heart, with all your soul, with all your mind, and with all your strength.' This is the first commandment.

"And the second, like it, is this: 'You shall love your neighbor as yourself.' There is no other commandment greater than these" (Mark 12:29-31).

As we have stated above, if you love the Lord your God with all your heart, soul, mind and strength, you will automatically keep the first four commandments. If you love God, you will never blaspheme against the Lord or curse Him. If you love him, you will never betray Him by making a blood covenant with an idol.

Likewise, if you love your neighbor as yourself, you will never murder your neighbor. If you love your neighbor as yourself, you will never steal from your neighbor. If you love your neighbor as yourself, you will not covet his possessions. If you love Him as yourself, you will be happy when God blesses him. You will not be jealous of him. If you love your neighbor as yourself, you will never try to take his wife for yourself.

This is why love is so important when it comes to keeping the Law of Moses. In the end, it is not the man who tries so hard to keep the law who will actually keep the law. In the end, only a man who has the true love of God in his heart will keep the Law of Moses.

This is written in the Bible:

For the entire law is fulfilled in keeping this one command: "Love your neighbor as yourself" (Galatians 5:14).

Owe no one anything except to love one another, for he who loves another has fulfilled the law.
For the commandments, "You shall not commit adultery," "You shall not murder," "You shall not steal," "You shall not bear false witness," "You shall not covet," and if there is any other commandment, are all summed up in this saying, namely, "You shall love your neighbor as yourself."
Love does no harm to a neighbor; therefore love is the fulfillment of the law (Romans 13:8-10).

To sum up, Jesus taught that the heart must change if one hopes to keep the Law of Moses. It is not enough for a person to change the outside. The inside must change. A person must have the real love of God to keep the law. The selfishness, anger, and bitterness that lives in a person's heart must be replaced by the genuine love of God. Only then can a person keep the law.

10 The Ninth Commandment

You shall not bear false witness against your neighbor (Exodus 20:16).

You shall not steal, nor deal falsely, nor lie to one another (Leviticus 19:11).

The ninth of the Ten Commandments in the Law of Moses is "You shall not bear false witness against your neighbor." In other words, you shall not lie about your neighbor or accuse him wrongly. It is also written in the Law of Moses, "You shall not steal, nor deal falsely, nor lie to one another."

Lies of all kinds are forbidden in the law of Moses. The worst kind of lie is one that wrongly accuses or harms a neighbor.

The Law of Moses also teaches about oaths. It is written in the Law, "If a man makes a vow to the Lord, or swears an oath to bind himself by some agreement, he shall not break his word; he shall do according to all that proceeds from his mouth" (Numbers 30:1-2).

Under the Law of Moses, an oath was considered to be unbreakable. It did not matter how difficult it was to keep an oath, it still needed to be kept. Under the Law of Moses, people feared God. They knew that if they broke their oath, God would be angered.

The value of an oath and a covenant can be seen in the story of Joshua and the city of Gibeon. When Joshua led the Israelites out of the wilderness into the land of Canaan, there was a city in Canaan known as Gibeon. The Gibeonites were Amorites. They were one of the tribes that Israel was supposed to completely destroy. This tribe committed all the evil deeds that the other Amorite tribes committed.

The Gibeonites knew that Joshua was called by God to destroy the Amorites. They knew that God had delivered Israel from Egypt and that the army of the Egyptians was destroyed in the Red Sea. They decided that their only hope was to convince Joshua that they were not Amorites. They decided to lie to Joshua, to try to convince him that they came from far away, and that they were not one of the nearby tribes that Joshua was supposed to destroy.

So the Gibeonites dressed in old clothes, and they put on worn-out sandals. They placed some dry and moldy bread in their packs. Then they approached Joshua and his army and said to him, "We have come from a distant land to make a covenant with you." At first, Joshua doubted that they actually came from far away. He suspected that they might actually live nearby, that they might actually be Amorites. But the men of Gibeon insisted that they were not Amorites. They declared they lived far away from the land of the Amorites. They showed him their worn clothes, and moldy bread. They told Joshua that their clothes had been like new when they began their voyage from their homeland, but they had traveled so far that their clothes had become worn out. And so Joshua was convinced. He made a covenant of peace with the men of Gibeon. He promised them that Israel would not destroy them, that their nation could enter into a peace treaty with Israel.

Later on, Joshua discovered that the Gibeonites had lied to him. They were Amorites! They lived nearby! They were one of the nations that the Israelites were supposed to destroy!

The men of Israel decided to keep their covenant with Gibeon. They said, "We have sworn to Gibeon by the Lord God of Israel, now therefore, we may not touch them." Gibeon had lied to Israel, but the men of Israel were not liars. They kept their promise of peace with Gibeon, and Gibeon was not destroyed. Instead, the Gibeonites were forced to gather firewood and carry water for the Israelites.

Many years later, one of the kings of Israel named Saul decided to break the covenant of peace between Israel and the Gibeonites. King Saul decided that because the Gibeonites were actually Amorites, God would be pleased with him if he killed them. And so many Gibeonites living near Israel were murdered by King Saul's men.

Famine and drought came to the land of Israel during the days of King David, the successor of King Saul. This famine lasted for three years. David prayed and asked the Lord why this drought had come. The Lord answered David, "It is because of Saul and his bloodthirsty house, because he killed the Gibeonites" (2 Samuel 21:1).

David went to the Gibeonites who had survived the crimes of Saul and said to them, "What shall I do for you? How can I pay the price for this great sin so that you will bless us?"

The Gibeonites asked that some of the descendants of Saul would be executed for what he had done. And so seven of Saul's descendants were turned over the Gibeonites, who put them to death. Then the famine came to an end.

Can you understand how important a promise was according to the Law of Moses? Joshua made a promise and a covenant with his enemies. Even though it was difficult, Joshua kept his covenant and his promise to the Amorites. Even though the Gibeonites had lied to him, Joshua refused to lie to them. He had promised that they would not be killed, and they were not killed.

Even God himself honored the promise and the covenant that Joshua made with Gibeon. King Saul thought that God would be pleased if he slaughtered the Gibeonites. God was not pleased! Instead of blessing Saul's action, God sent famine to the land of Israel, because Israel had broken its covenant and its promise to the people of Gibeon.

Under the Law of Moses, the principal of judgment was "an eye for an eye and a tooth for a tooth." King Saul had murdered the Gibeonites, so the Gibeonites were allowed to take their revenge against the descendants of King Saul. Seven descendants of King Saul gave their lives because of the sin that Saul had committed.

Why is it so important that people keep their promises? God keeps His promises, and His people must keep their promises.

Jesus spoke about Satan, "He was a murderer from the beginning and does not stand in the truth because there is no truth in him. When he speaks a lie, he speaks from his own resources, for he is a liar and the father of it" (John 8:44).

Satan is the father of lies. Satan cannot tell the truth, because there is no truth in him. His heart is full of lies, and everything that he says is a lie.

God cannot tell a lie. His words are always true, and there is no deceit in them. The Spirit of God is called the Spirit of Truth. The children of God must learn to love the truth and speak the truth. Liars will lie, but men of God will always keep their word.

The Bible reveals that hell is a lake of fire. The Bible teaches us that all liars will be cast into the lake of fire.

"But the cowardly, unbelieving, abominable, murderers, sexually immoral, sorcerers, idolaters, and all liars shall have their part in the lake which burns with fire and brimstone, which is the second death" (Revelation 21:8).

JESUS AND THE NINTH COMMANDMENT

Jesus never told a lie. He taught his followers to always speak the truth from a good heart. He taught them not to make oaths but to simply speak the truth at all times. He said, "Let your 'Yes' be 'Yes,' and your 'No,' 'No.' For whatever is more than these is from the evil one" (Matthew 5:37).

Jesus always taught that if a man's heart is good, then his words will also be true and good. A man's words come from his heart. Whatever is in a man's heart will come out of his mouth when he speaks. An evil man cannot actually say anything good. His words are coming from an evil heart. Even when he says words that sound good, those words are still coming from an evil heart.

Jesus said to the Pharisees, "Brood of vipers! How can you, being evil, speak good things? For out of the abundance of the heart the mouth speaks. A good man out of the good treasure of his heart brings forth good things, and an evil man out of the evil treasure brings forth evil things. But I say to you that for every idle word men may speak, they will give account of it in the day of judgment. For by your words you will be justified, and by your words you will be condemned" (Matthew 12:34-37).

Jesus is teaching that on the Day of Judgment, every word that a man has ever spoken will be reviewed in the presence of God. When every word is reviewed and judged, God will expose not only the words that were spoken, but also what was in the heart of a man when he spoke those words. If a man greeted his neighbor with friendly words, but he hated that neighbor in his heart, he will be judged for those words as if he had cursed his neighbor. Likewise, a good man, with a heart filled with the love of God, will speak good words, and he will be rewarded by God on the Day of Judgment.

11 The Tenth Commandment

"You shall not covet your neighbor's house; you shall not covet your neighbor's wife, nor his male servant, nor his female servant, nor his ox, nor his donkey, nor anything that is your neighbor's" (Exodus 20:17).

Covetousness is a sin of the heart. It is a hidden sin, a sin that cannot easily be seen by other people. It is a sin that is seen by God.

God knows what is in your heart. If you lust after a woman, God knows it, and your desire for that woman is like adultery in His sight. If you lust after gold, or glory, or the praise of man, or success, all those things are clearly seen by God.

The only way to keep from coveting is to have a heart filled with the love of God. If you love the Lord your God with all your heart, soul, mind and strength, then no idol can live in your heart. Nothing will be able to take the place of God in your heart. If you love your neighbor as yourself, it will be impossible for you to covet your neighbor's possessions. If he has a new car, you will be happy that he has it! You will be just as happy if he has a new car as you would be if you received a new car, because you love him as yourself! If you love your neighbor, how can you covet his wife or his possessions?

Covetousness is closely related to other sins of the heart. Covetousness is closely related to greed and lust. Covetousness works together with jealousy. When you covet the possession of a neighbor, you are likely to become jealous of that neighbor.

Covetousness leads to other sins. If you covet a neighbor's possession, you will begin to think about how you can take that possession for yourself. Your covetousness might cause you to steal from your neighbor. If you covet your neighbor's wife, you might become tempted to commit adultery with that woman.

Jesus taught about covetousness (Luke 12:13-34). A man came to Jesus and said to him, "Teacher, tell my brother to divide the inheritance with me."

Jesus warned the man severely. He told him, "Watch out and beware of covetousness. For a man's life 'does not consist in the abundance of his possessions.'" Life is not measured by how much you own.

Jesus knew that this man was so focused on receiving his inheritance, that he was in danger of missing the Kingdom of God. A great prophet was right in front of him, teaching him the way to eternal life. But the only thing this man could think about was his inheritance. Even as he stood before the Messiah, his only thought was that maybe Jesus could help him get his inheritance from his brother. All day long he thought about his inheritance. His heart was full of bitter thoughts about his brother who had cheated him.

After warning the man, Jesus told him a parable about a rich man:

A rich man had a fertile farm that produced fine crops. He said to himself, "What should I do? I don't have room for all my crops." Then he said, 'I know! I'll tear down my barns and build bigger ones. Then I'll have room enough to store all my wheat and other goods. And I'll sit back and say to myself, "My friend, you have enough stored away for years to come. Now take it easy! Eat, drink, and be merry!"
But God said to him, "You fool! You will die this very night. Then who will get everything you worked for?"
Yes, a person is a fool to store up earthly wealth but not have a rich relationship with God.

In this parable, a rich man put his trust in the wealth that was stored in his barns. He put his trust in something that seemed valuable and secure. In fact, that man's wealth could not save him from death or from hell.

Wealth can easily become an idol of the heart. It can become something that men trust in and rely upon, instead of trusting in God. Like every idol, it is useless. It cannot save you when trouble comes.

In fact, the Injil states that covetousness and idolatry are actually the same thing. When you deeply desire and covet something, that thing becomes an idol in your heart. This is why Paul wrote in the Bible that covetousness and idolatry are the same thing.

Therefore put to death your members which are on the earth: fornication, uncleanness, passion, evil desire, and covetousness, which is idolatry (Colossians 3:5-6).

Therefore, the commandment not to covet is actually a commandment concerning idolatry. It is not speaking about idols of wood and stone. It is speaking about idols that live in men's hearts. A man's idol might be his wealth, or his education, or even his family. His idols might be good things. But when a man puts his trust in those good things they become idols and they will fail him in the end.

The desires of a man's flesh can also become idols in his heart. It is said there are three main desires of the flesh that grow in a man's heart. These three things are known as the three g's: gold, girls, and glory. Men desire wealth. They desire women, and they desire glory, the praise of man. The lust for these things is the lust of the flesh. It is covetousness, and it is idolatry. The man who chases after these desires is a covetous man.

When the desires of your heart consume you, they have become idols. When you are hungry, you eat and feel satisfied. But when covetousness fills your heart, the more you get, the more you desire. If you covet money, you will never be satisfied no matter how much money you receive. Money will become an idol in your heart, and you will always desire more money. If you covet power and glory, it will not matter how much honor men give you. You will always desire more. The sin of covetousness is a hungry sin. A covetous man is never satisfied.

Covetousness is idolatry. It is putting your desire upon something other than God and putting your trust in something other than God.

12 The Seventh Commandment

We have not yet studied the seventh commandment given to Moses: "You shall not commit adultery." Under the Law of Moses, the penalty for committing adultery was death. Consider the following scriptures written by Moses:

> **The man who commits adultery with another man's wife, he who commits adultery with his neighbor's wife, the adulterer and the adulteress, shall surely be put to death (Leviticus 20:10).**

> **The man who lies with his father's wife has uncovered his father's nakedness; both of them shall surely be put to death. Their blood shall be upon them (Leviticus 20:11).**

> **If a man is found lying with a woman married to a husband, then both of them shall die—the man that lay with the woman, and the woman; so you shall put away the evil from Israel (Deuteronomy 22:22).**

> **If a man lies with his daughter-in-law, both of them shall surely be put to death. They have committed perversion. Their blood shall be upon them (Leviticus 20:12).**

When Jesus taught about adultery, he taught that adultery begins in the heart of man. Jesus taught that when a man lusts after a woman who is not his wife, that man has already committed adultery in his heart.

Jesus said, "I say to you that whoever looks at a woman to lust for her has already committed adultery with her in his heart" (Matthew 5:28).

This might seem like a very difficult teaching. Which man has never lusted after a woman? Nevertheless, lust is sin. In the eyes of God, it is the same as the sin of adultery. Just because lust is such a common sin does not make that sin less serious in the eyes of God. Even if every man on earth has lusted after a woman, lust would still be a sin.

Sin is not determined by what is normal in the eyes of man. Sin is determined by the righteousness of God. Everything that falls short of that righteousness is sin. Many things that seem normal and honorable in the sight of men are abominations in the sight of God.

Jesus said to the Pharisees, "You are those who justify yourselves before men, but God knows your hearts. For what is highly esteemed among men is an abomination in the sight of God" (Luke 16:15).

The teachings of Jesus are clear. The man who lusts after a woman has committed adultery with that woman in his heart. Under the law of Moses, the penalty for adultery was death. Jesus taught about a much higher penalty.

The righteousness of God is a terrifying thing. God is holy, and men are corrupted by sin. God is holy, and men's hearts are full of lust and uncleanness. God's holiness makes it difficult for a man to escape his sin and live with God forever. Nonetheless, there is a road that leads to life.

THE COVENANT OF MARRIAGE

God keeps His covenants. He honors the covenant that He made with Abraham to this very day. He told Abraham, "… Blessing I will bless you, and multiplying I will multiply your descendants as the stars of the heaven and as the sand which is on the seashore" (Genesis 22:17). Even today that blessing continues to work.

In the Torah, the very first covenant that God speaks about is the covenant of marriage. In marriage, two become one. In marriage, a man leaves his father and mother, and is united with his wife, and the two become one flesh. Marriage is a holy covenant.

The covenant of marriage has a high cost. When you marry someone, the rest of your life belongs to that person. You are no longer free to do whatever you want. You are connected to that person, and only death can break that connection.

Marriage is created by God. It is God who declared that a man shall leave his father and mother and be united with his wife, and that the two should become one flesh. When you study the teachings of Jesus, it becomes clear that God never wanted divorce to enter this earth.

The Pharisees tried to justify divorce using the words of Moses, saying, "Moses permitted a man to write a certificate of divorce, and to dismiss his wife."

Jesus answered and said to them, "Because of the hardness of your heart he wrote you this precept. But from the beginning of the creation, God **'made them male and female. For this reason a man shall leave his father and mother and be joined to his wife and the two shall become one flesh'**; so then they are no longer two, but one flesh. Therefore what God has joined together, let not man separate."

After leaving the Pharisees, Jesus continued to teach his disciples with the words, "And I say to you, whoever divorces his wife, except for sexual immorality, and marries another, commits adultery; and whoever marries her who is divorced commits adultery" (Matthew 19:3-9).

Jesus made it clear that divorce was a sin. Moses allowed divorce to take place because men's hearts were hardened and evil, but God originally intended marriage to be a lifetime commitment between a man and a woman.

The prophet Malachi who prophesied the coming of Jesus, spoke this way "Let none deal treacherously with the wife of his youth. For the LORD God of Israel says that He hates divorce, for it covers one's garment with violence" (Malachi 2:16).

Divorce is violence. When a man divorces his wife, he destroys the life of his wife. Divorce tears apart something that God has put together. Divorce tears apart the blood covenant that is formed between a man and his wife.

A man might feel very justified in divorcing his wife and marrying another wife, but Jesus taught that doing so is actually a form of adultery. "Whoever divorces his wife, except for sexual immorality, and marries another, commits adultery." Likewise, Jesus taught that whoever marries a divorced woman also commits adultery.

If God hates divorce so much, why did he permit it in the Law of Moses? In fact, the law that came through Moses was only a partial law, an incomplete law. The true righteousness of God is revealed in the ministry of Jesus. In the teachings of Jesus, we see a more complete picture of the righteousness of God and the heart of God. The teachings of Jesus reveal the heart of God. They reveal the righteousness of God, the character of God, and the love of God.

The Christian Bible speaks about the Law of Moses with these words: "For the law, having a shadow of the good things to come, and not the very image of the things, can never with these same sacrifices, which they offer continually year by year, make those who approach perfect" (Hebrews 10:1).

Another passage describes the law of Moses in this way: "So let no one judge you in food or in drink, or regarding a festival or a new moon or Sabbaths, which are a shadow of things to come, but the substance is of Christ" (Colossians 2:16-17).

In other words, the perfection of God is not found in the Law of Moses. The perfection of God is found in the teachings and ministry of Jesus. The Law of Moses, and the religious rituals that are found in that law, only show us a "shadow" of the true righteousness of God. The real righteousness of God is found in the life, ministry, and teachings of Jesus.

The sacrifices of sheep, goats, and cattle that are required under the Law of Moses can never completely pay the price of sin. They can never make the ones offering the sacrifices perfect in the sight of God. They are only a "shadow" of the perfect sacrifice that makes it possible for men to be completely delivered from the power of death and sin.

A WOMAN CAUGHT IN ADULTERY

Under the Law of Moses, the penalty for adultery was death. Jesus taught that even when a man lusted after a woman, he had already committed adultery with her in his heart. Jesus taught that the penalty for sin was much higher than death, it was an eternal punishment.

Although Jesus exposed the sinfulness of man and the price of sin more clearly than any other prophet, He also displayed the love of God. He taught that men should even love their enemies. He taught that God deeply loved mankind, at a level that is beyond human understanding.

How is it possible to teach the righteousness of God in such a way that every man is condemned to eternal punishment and at the same time teach about a love that is greater than any man can understand? If God loves mankind so deeply, can he condemn everyone to hell? Every person has sinned, and the price of sin is death and hell (the second death). And yet Jesus taught of a narrow road that leads to life. What is this road? How can a person walk upon it?

One day the Pharisees caught a woman and a man in the act of committing adultery (John 8). According to the Law of Moses, this woman and man needed to be condemned to death. The Pharisees dragged the woman to where Jesus was preaching. They knew that Jesus preached much about the love of God. They wanted to see if Jesus would actually keep the Law of Moses and condemn this woman to death as the Law required. If Jesus refused to condemn the woman, then the Pharisees could accuse Jesus of breaking the Law of Moses. The penalty for breaking the Law of Moses was death.

And so, the woman was dragged before Jesus. The Pharisees said to Jesus "Teacher, this woman was caught in adultery, in the very act. Now Moses, in the law, commanded us that such should be stoned. But what do You say?"

Jesus ignored the Pharisees and their questions. He stooped down and wrote in the dust with His finger, acting as if He had not even heard them. The Pharisees became more aggressive with their questions, demanding that Jesus give them an answer. Finally, Jesus stood up and said to them, "He who is without sin among you, let him throw a stone at her first." Again, He stooped down and wrote in the ground.

Something strange began to happen. The Pharisees and their followers became very quiet, as each man thought of the sins that he had committed. It was true that the woman who was caught committing adultery was a sinner and deserved to die. It was also true that every man who accused her had also committed sins deserving of death. Every man had broken the Sabbath at some point in his life. Some had stolen from their neighbors; others had committed adultery. Most had lied. Some had dishonored and disobeyed their parents.

As each man remembered his own sins, he became fearful. Somehow he knew that if he lifted a hand against this woman, he was putting himself in danger. The one who judges others is judged in the same way that he has judged them. The one who judges others without mercy will also be judged without mercy. This is a principal found throughout the Torah and the Injil.

For judgment is without mercy to the one who has shown no mercy. Mercy triumphs over judgment (James 2:13).

And so the men began to walk away, one by one. The mob that was looking forward to bloodshed disappeared within just a few minutes. Jesus was still writing on the ground. Finally, He looked up, and saw that He was alone with the adulterous woman. He said to her, "Woman, where are those accusers of yours? Has no one condemned you?"

She said, "No one, Lord." And Jesus said to her, "Neither do I condemn you; go and sin no more."

In this story, we see how Jesus treated a woman who deserved the judgment of God. Under the Law of Moses, she deserved to be stoned to death. According to the teachings of Jesus, she deserved eternal punishment.

WHO IS ABLE TO JUDGE?

But who is able to judge this woman and give her the punishment for her sins that she deserves? Can a sinner judge a sinner? When a sinner judges a sinner, the one who is doing the judging must also be judged! If the Pharisees truly wanted to carry out the judgments found in the Law of Moses, then after stoning the woman to death they should have stoned each other to death as well!

This is the problem with the Law of Moses. Everyone is condemned by the Law of Moses. Everyone has lied. Everyone has broken the Sabbath. Everyone has experienced lust in his heart. Everyone has dishonored their parents at some point in his life. Who is innocent of these things? Who is perfect as God is perfect?

There is only one man that both the Quran and the Injil testify about as being sinless. This man is not Mohammed. The sins of Mohammed are spoken of several times in the Quran. If you believe that the Quran is the direct word of God, then you must also believe that Mohammed was a sinner!

> That Allah **may forgive thee of thy sin** that which is past and that which is to come, and may perfect His favor unto thee, and may guide thee on a right path (Quran 48:2, Pickthal).

> Then have patience (O Muhammad). Lo! the promise of Allah is true. And **ask forgiveness of thy sin,** and hymn the praise of thy Lord at fall of night and in the early hours (Quran 40:55 Pickthal).

> So know (O Muhammad) that there is no Allah save Allah, and **ask forgiveness for thy sin** and for believing men and believing women. Allah knoweth (both) your place of turmoil and your place of rest (Quran 47:19, Pickthal).

Mohammed confessed his sins in the following hadiths:

> "By Allah! **I ask for forgiveness from Allah and turn to Him in repentance more than 70 times a day**" (Bukhari 8:319).

> "O Allah! **Set me apart from my sins as the East and West are set apart from each other and clean me from sins as a white garment is cleaned of dirt (after thorough washing). O Allah! Wash off my sins with water, snow and hail**" (Bukhari 1:711).

> O Allah! **Forgive me my sins that I did in the past or will do in the future, and also the sins I did in secret or in public**" (Bukhari 9:482).

There is only one man that Islamic scriptures and Christians speak of as being without sin. That man is Jesus. There was something very, very special about Jesus. No other prophet revealed the holiness of God in the way that Jesus did. No other prophet walked in sinless perfection the way that Jesus did. No other prophet has the right to judge sinners, because the scriptures testify that the prophets were also sinners.

Both Mohammed and the Torah spoke of the sins of Adam, the sins of Noah, the sins of Moses, and the sins of Abraham. Mohammed spoke about the anger that God will show towards the sin of these men on the Judgment Day (Bukhari 6:236). The Torah explains the sins of each of these men in much detail. Adam disobeyed God and ate the fruit from the tree of the knowledge of good and evil. Moses disobeyed God and struck the rock instead of speaking to it. Noah became drunk on wine. Abraham lied to King Abimelech.

These great prophets were not without sin. Therefore, they are not qualified to judge the sin of other men. These men needed a perfect sacrifice to escape from their sin. They needed to find the narrow road that leads to life, or they too would have been destroyed by their sin.

Neither Mohammed nor the Christian Bible ever speaks of the sin of Jesus. Mohammed testified, "There is none born among the off-spring of Adam, but Satan touches it. A child therefore, cries loudly at the time of birth because of the touch of Satan, except Mary and her child" (Bukhari 4:641, also 4:506).

With these words, Mohammed testified that Satan was unable to touch Jesus. Jesus is completely free from Satan's grasp, because Jesus is free from sin. It is the sin and evil covenants of mankind that give Satan the ability to control people's lives.

The devil tried to find sin in Jesus, but he failed. Jesus spent 40 days praying and fasting in the desert. At the end of this time, the devil came to tempt Jesus. Jesus passed the test. He refused to compromise with the devil at all. He refused to leave the path that God had set before him. The story of the temptation of Jesus is found in Matthew 4:1-11 and Luke 4:1-13.

Other passages in the Christian Bible also speak of the sinlessness of Jesus. Consider the following verses:

For to this you were called, because Christ also suffered for us, leaving us an example, that you should follow His steps: "Who

committed no sin, nor was deceit found in his mouth"(1 Peter 2:21-22).

And you know that He was manifested to take away our sins, and in Him there is no sin (1 John 3:5).

Which of you convicts Me of sin? And if I tell the truth, why do you not believe Me ? (John 8:46)

When the woman caught in adultery was brought before Jesus, there was only one person who could have condemned her. There was only one man who was without sin. That man was Jesus. Jesus could have condemned the woman, and her condemnation would have been deserved.

Instead of condemning her, Jesus showed her mercy. He refused to condemn her at that time. Instead of condemning her, Jesus said to her "Go and sin no more."

13 You Shall Not Commit Adultery

The story of Jesus and the adulterous woman is very similar to a story from the life of Mohammed. Like Jesus, Mohammed was asked to judge a couple caught in adultery. We can learn much about Mohammed by examining this story.

Two Jews were brought before Mohammed and were accused of committing adultery. Mohammed asked them "What is the legal punishment for this sin found in the Torah (Law of Moses)." The Jews lied to Mohammed. They told him that the Torah required that those who committed adultery should have their faces blackened and that they should be publicly humiliated. In fact, the Torah required death for adulterers and adulteresses.

A Torah was brought before Mohammed, and one of the Jews began reading from it regarding adultery. As he read, he covered the part of the Torah that spoke about the death penalty with his thumb, trying to hide from Mohammed what the Torah said. One of the Muslims saw what he was doing, and ordered him to lift up his hand to read what had been covered up. He lifted his hand, and the penalty for adultery was read before the Muslims. Mohammed applied the Law of Moses, and ordered that the adulterer and the adulteress be stoned to death. And so it was done.

"Narrated Ibn Umar (RA): A Jew and a Jewess were brought to Allah's Apostle (S) on a charge of committing illegal sexual intercourse. The Prophet asked them: 'What is the legal punishment (for this sin) in your Book (Torah)?' They replied: 'Our priests have innovated the blackening of faces with charcoal and Tajbiya' (being mounted on a donkey, with their faces in opposite directions, then mortified in public). Abdullah bin Salaam said: 'O Allah's Apostle, tell them to bring the Torah.' The Torah was brought, and then one of the Jews put his hand over the Divine Verse of the Rajm (stoning to death) and started reading what preceded and what followed it. On that, Ibn Salaam said to the Jew: 'Lift up your hand.' The Divine Verse of the Rajm was under his hand. So Allah's Apostle (S) ordered that the two (sinners) be stoned to death, and so they were stoned" (Bukhari 8:809).

Jesus was asked to condemn the adulterous women with the law of Moses. Instead of condemning her, Jesus told the adulterous woman "Go and sin no more." With these words, Jesus gave the woman an opportunity to change her life before she faced the judgment of God on the last day.

In contrast, Mohammed condemned an adulterous woman and her partner using the Law of Moses, and they were stoned to death. In these stories, we can clearly see the difference between Jesus and Mohammed.

When we read the Quran and the hadiths, it becomes very clear that Mohammed judged sinners. Many sinners were condemned to death by Mohammed. These sinners were lawbreakers, and they deserved to die according to the Law of Moses.

But what about Mohammed himself? If Mohammed was also a sinner, how could he judge sinners? Did God make an exception in the case of Mohammed? Did God allow Mohammed to judge sinners even though Mohammed had also sinned? Did God forgive Mohammed's sins and allow him to judge the sins of others?

The teachings of Jesus are very clear. In the same way you have judged others, you will be judged. Mohammed used the Law of Moses to judge an adulterer and an adulteress, and he ordered that they be stoned to death. Just as Mohammed used the Law of Moses to condemn these two people, Mohammed will also be judged by the Law of Moses. This is the justice of God.

What does the Law of Moses say about Mohammed? In this part of the book we will look at the life and teachings of Mohammed. In particular, we will look at the life and teachings of Mohammed in relation to the Law of Moses and the teachings of Jesus. If we look at Mohammed's life in this way, it will become very clear what kind of a man Mohammed was. His character will be clearly seen. It will become possible to better understand the revelations that he received, and the judgments that he made.

THE TEST OF A TRUE PROPHET

Mohammed's ministry followed the ministry of Moses and Jesus. When God sends a prophet, that prophet brings a fresh revelation to the earth. God will never send a prophet who leads people into bondage and sin. He will only send prophets who help people to leave their sin and draw closer to God.

True prophets build upon the ministry of former prophets. Moses taught the laws of God and revealed a "shadow" of God's righteousness and holiness. Jesus raised the standard. He walked in the character and perfection of God. He not only taught about the righteousness of God, He demonstrated the love of God and the righteousness of God to the earth. The teachings of Jesus carry greater authority than the teachings of Moses, because Jesus lived up to the standard of righteousness found in the Law of Moses and went beyond it.

As we study the life of Mohammed, one of two things will happen. Muslims believe that the life and teachings of Mohammed carry even greater weight than the life and teachings of Moses and Jesus. If Mohammed is a true prophet sent by God, the life of God and the holiness of God will be seen in his life and ministry at a very high degree. In fact, if Mohammed is a true prophet whose teachings carry greater authority than the teachings of Jesus, Mohammed will bring a greater revelation of God's righteousness and holiness to the earth than Jesus did. Not only will he teach a higher level of righteousness, he will demonstrate that righteousness in his life to a greater degree than Jesus did. If Mohammed did this, then surely he had the right to bring God's judgment to sinners and evildoers. If Mohammed did this, then surely his teachings have greater authority than the teachings of Jesus

Something else might happen as we study the life and teachings of Mohammed in relation to the Law of Moses and the teachings of Jesus. If Mohammed was not a true prophet who taught and demonstrated a greater righteousness than Jesus did, then the life and teachings of Jesus will expose Mohammed and condemn him.

MOHAMMED AND DIVORCE

We have already examined the teachings of the Law of Moses concerning adultery and divorce, and the teachings of Jesus. Jesus taught that those who divorced and remarried (except in cases of marital unfaithfulness) were guilty of adultery. What did Mohammed teach and practice concerning divorce?

In some cases, Mohammed taught that Allah hates divorce. In this way his teachings seem to be similar to the teachings of Jesus and Moses. Consider the following hadiths:

> Narrated Muharib: The Prophet said: Allah did not make anything lawful more abominable to Him than divorce (Abu Dawud 2172).

> Narrated Abdullah ibn Umar: The Prophet said: Of all the lawful acts the most detestable to Allah is divorce (Abu Dawud 2173).

Although Mohammed condemns divorce in these hadiths, there is more to the story. Mohammed made it very easy for Muslims to get divorced. In Islam, a husband needs only to speak the word *talaq* three times to divorce his wife. The first two times he speaks this word, he can change his mind and reconcile with his wife. After speaking it the third time, he cannot remarry his wife unless she first marries and divorces another man first. Usually a waiting period is required after each time that *talaq* is spoken.

If one studies the life of Mohammed, it becomes clear that Mohammed's wives feared divorce, even though they were faithful to him. This is seen in the following hadith:

... When Sauda daughter of Zam'ah became old and feared that the Apostle of Allah would divorce her, she said: Apostle of Allah, I give to 'A'ishah the day you visit me. The Apostle of Allah accepted it from her. She said: We think that Allah, the Exalted, revealed about this or a similar matter in the Quran: "If a wife fears cruelty or desertion on her husband's part" (Sunan Abu Dawud Volume 2 Book V 705).

Aisha: Never did I find any woman more loving to me than Sauda bint Zam'a (Muslim 3451).

In this story, Sauda, one of Mohammed's wives, began to fear that Mohammed was going to divorce her. According to Aisha, Mohammed's favorite wife, Sauda was a very loving woman, a woman who showed Aisha more love than any other. (Muslim 8:3451) Aisha also reported that Sauda was "a huge fat lady." (Bukhari 6:318) Quite simply, Sauda had become old and unattractive to Mohammed, and she began to fear that Mohammed would soon divorce her, because he was no longer attracted to her. In order to stop the divorce from taking place, Sauda made an agreement with Mohammed. Mohammed used to spend each night at the home of one of his wives. Sauda agreed to give her "turn" with Mohammed to Aisha, Mohammed's favorite wife. By doing this, she hoped to gain favor with Mohammed and avoid the divorce. Mohammed agreed to keep Sauda as his wife, and he received the following revelation which was written in the Quran:

If a wife fears cruelty or desertion on her husband's part, there is no blame on them if they arrange an amicable settlement between themselves; and such settlement is best; even though men's souls are swayed by greed. But if ye do good and practice self-restraint, Allah is well-acquainted with all that ye do (Quran 4:128 YUSUFALI).

This revelation made it clear that God supported the agreement that Mohammed made with Sauda. Mohammed did not have to sleep with her any more, and she no longer feared that Mohammed would divorce her.

The Sunni scholar Ibn Kathir wrote:

"Making peace is better than separation. An example of such peace can be felt in the story of Sauda bint Zam'ah who when she became aged, the prophet wanted to divorce her, but she made peace with him by offering the night he used to spend with her to Aisha so that he would keep her. The Prophet accepted such terms and kept her."

On another occasion Mohammed had a severe disagreement with his wives because one of them told something that he did not want the other wives to know. When the other wives heard the secret, they became enraged at Mohammed. The dispute was so serious that people thought that Mohammed would divorce his wives. Mohammed received the following revelation from Allah that is written in the Quran:

> "The prophet had trusted some of his wives with a certain statement, then one of them spread it, and GOD let him know about it. He then informed his wife of part of the issue, and disregarded part. She asked him, "Who informed you of this?" He said, "I was informed by the Omniscient, Most Cognizant."
>
> If the two of you repent to GOD, then your hearts have listened. But if you band together against him, then GOD is his ally, and so is Gabriel and the righteous believers. Also, the angels are his helpers.
>
> If he divorces you, his Lord will substitute other wives in your place who are better than you; submitters (Muslims), believers (Mu'mins), obedient, repentant, worshipers, pious, either previously married, or virgins.
>
> O you who believe, protect yourselves and your families from the Hellfire whose fuel is people and rocks. Guarding it are stern and powerful angels who never disobey GOD; they do whatever they are commanded to do" (Quran 66:3-6 Rashad).

This passage from the Quran shows that Mohammed would have been justified in divorcing his wives for telling his secret. Allah would have supported him in this decision and would have replaced the wives that he divorced with better wives who were more obedient and better Muslims. The wives that he divorced would have been in danger of hell fire.

Therefore, if we look at the example of Mohammed's life, the legitimate reasons for a man to divorce his wife become clear. If a woman tells her husband's secret, he has grounds to divorce her. Allah will support him and give him a better wife to replace her. Likewise, if a woman becomes old and unattractive, her husband may want to divorce her, as Mohammed did Sauda. Mohammed was in no way rebuked for wishing to divorce Sauda, but Allah was pleased when Sauda found another solution. Therefore, if the unwanted wife can make an agreement with her husband so that he agrees not to divorce her so long as she no longer expects him to sleep with her, it is a good solution according to the revelations of Mohammed

It seems that the teachings of Jesus in this area are quite different from the revelations of Mohammed. According to the teachings of Jesus, the only legitimate cause of divorce is sexual immorality. In these two cases, nobody accused Mohammed's wives of committing sexual immorality, so divorce would not have been justified in either case. However, the revelations that Mohammed received from Allah indicate that Allah would have supported Mohammed if he had decided to go ahead and divorce his wives.

MUT'A MARRIAGES

When Mohammed's men were at war, divorce and remarriage were made very, very easy for them. There was a time when Mohammed's men were separated from their wives for many days when they had gone out for battle. In frustration, they came to Mohammed and asked him, "Shall we castrate ourselves?" Mohammed then allowed his men to enter into temporary marriages (Mut'a) with the women of the area. These marriages typically lasted for three nights, to satisfy the sexual desires of the soldiers. When the three nights were up, the women were usually divorced. Later on, Mohammed forbade this kind of marriage.

> Narrated Abdullah: We used to participate in the holy wars carried on by the Prophet and we had no women (wives) with us. So we said (to the Prophet). "Shall we castrate ourselves?" But the Prophet forbade us to do that and thenceforth he allowed us to marry a woman (temporarily) by giving her even a garment, and then he recited: "O you who believe! Do not make unlawful the good things which Allah has made lawful for you" (Bukhari 6:139).

> Narrated Jabir bin 'Abdullah and Salama bin Al-Akwa': While we were in an army, Allah's Apostle came to us and said, "You have been allowed to do the Mut'a (marriage), so do it." Salama bin Al-Akwa' said: Allah's Apostle's said, "If a man and a woman agree (to marry temporarily), their marriage should last for three nights, and if they like to continue, they can do so; and if they want to separate, they can do

so." I do not know whether that was only for us or for all the people in general. Abu Abdullah (Al-Bukhari) said: 'Ali made it clear that the Prophet said, "The Mut'a marriage has been cancelled (made unlawful)" (Bukhari 7:52).

MOHAMMED AND ZAID

Mohammed had an adopted son, Zaid. Originally, Zaid was the slave of Mohammed's first wife Khadijah. When Khadijah married Mohammed, she gave Zaid to Mohammed as a wedding present. Mohammed developed a close relationship with Zaid, and eventually adopted him. He took him to the Kaaba and announced to everyone, "Witness that Zaid becomes my son, with mutual rights of inheritance." Therefore, Zaid became known as "Zaid ibn Muhammad", Zaid the son of Mohammed.

In 625 AD Mohammed arranged a marriage between his cousin, Zaynab, and his adopted son Zaid. One day Mohammed came to Zaid's house to speak with him. Zaid was not at home, but his wife Zaynab was in the house, dressed only in her undergarments. Mohammed caught a glimpse of her as he stood at the door. When Zaynab saw that Mohammed was at the door, she immediately jumped up, dressed herself properly, and invited Mohammed into the house. Mohammed refused her invitation and turned away from her and left the house. As he did so, he muttered, "Praise be to Allah, who turns the hearts of men!"

When Zaynab's husband returned to his home, Zaynab told him about Mohammed's visit. Zaid asked Zaynab why she had not invited Mohammed into their home. Zaynab replied that she had invited Mohammed to enter, but that he refused. Zaid asked her if Mohammed said anything to her. Zaynab replied, "When he turned away from me, I heard him say something that I could hardly understand. I heard him say, "Praise be to Allah who turns the hearts of men."

Zaid knew Mohammed very well and understood what had happened. He suspected that Mohammed desired his wife. Zaid greatly respected Mohammed, so much so that he could not think of keeping his wife for himself if Mohammed desired to have her.

Zaid came to Mohammed and said to him, "O Messenger of God, I learned that you came to my house…. Perhaps you liked Zaynab. I can leave her." (Ibn Sa`d and al-Tabari)

Mohammed refused Zaid's offer, saying to him, 'Keep your wife to thyself and fear God.'

Zaid felt very uneasy about his marriage to Zaynab. Zaid owed everything he had to Mohammed, and he was convinced that Mohammed desired his wife. To fix the situation, Zaid decided to divorce his wife so that Mohammed could do what he wanted to do.

And so, Zaid and Zaynab were divorced. After the waiting period of three months had passed, Mohammed called Zaid and said to him, 'I have no one whom I trust more than you; therefore, seek the hand of Zaynab for me!' Zaid went to his former wife as she was praying in the mosque and told her of Mohammed's request of marriage.

Zaynab replied to Zaid, "I do not do anything until I solicit the will of my Lord." She remained praying in the mosque. Allah quickly revealed his will to Mohammed (Muslim 3330). While Zaynab was still praying, Mohammed received the following revelation from Allah:

> "And when you said to him to whom Allah had shown favor and to whom you had shown a favor: Keep your wife to yourself and be careful of (your duty to) Allah; and you concealed in your soul what Allah would bring to light, and you feared men, and Allah had a greater right that you should fear Him. But when Zaid had accomplished his want of her, We gave her to you as a wife, so that there should be no difficulty for the believers in respect of the wives of their adopted sons, when they have accomplished their want of them; and Allah's command shall be performed" (Quran 33:37, Shakir).

In this revelation, Allah rebukes Mohammed for telling Zaid to keep his wife, because when Mohammed said this to Zaid, he already knew in his heart what Allah wanted. Allah wanted Zaynab to become Mohammed's wife. It was Allah who placed the desire for Zaynab in Mohammed's heart. It was Allah who wanted Zaid to divorce Zaynab so that Mohammed could marry her. It was Allah who gave Zaynab to Mohammed as his wife.

Who can oppose the will of God? When Zaynab heard about the revelation that Mohammed had received, she agreed to marry him. In fact, she boasted about her marriage to Mohammed's other wives, saying, "Allah married me to the prophet in the Heavens" (Bukhari 9:517).

It is written in the Law of Moses, "If a man lies with his daughter-in-law, both of them shall surely be put to death. They have committed perversion. Their blood shall be upon them" (Leviticus 20:12).

If Zaid was actually Mohammed's son, then what took place was a very serious sin indeed. If Zaid was Mohammed's son, then Mohammed was guilty of sexual relations with his daughter-in-law.

Fortunately for Mohammed, he soon received the revelation that adopted sons were not real sons in the sight of God. Therefore, adopted sons should be called by the name of their real father, not the name of the one who adopted them. It is written in the Quran: "Nor has He (Allah) made your adopted sons your sons. Such is (only) your (manner of) speech by your mouths. But God tells the truth, and He shows the way. Call them by (the names of) their fathers, that is better in the sight of God" (Quran 33:5).

Why did Allah want Mohammed to marry Zaynab? This is also explained in the Quran. Allah wanted Mohammed to marry Zaynab "so that there should be no difficulty for the believers in respect of the wives of their adopted sons, when they have accomplished their want of them" (Quran 33:37). In other words, the reason that Allah wanted Mohammed to marry the wife of his adopted son was so that Muslim men would know that they were free to marry the wives of their adopted sons if their adopted sons decided to divorce their wives.

This seems to contradict the teachings of Jesus, even if an adopted son is not seen as a real son in the sight of God. Jesus taught, "Whoever divorces his wife and marries another commits adultery; and whoever marries her who is divorced from her husband commits adultery" (Luke 16:18). Even if Zaid was not a true son of Mohammed, he certainly divorced his wife, and Mohammed married her. According to the teachings of Jesus, this is adultery.

DOES LUST COME FROM GOD?

Jesus taught, "Whoever looks at a woman to lust for her has already committed adultery with her in his heart" (Matthew 5:28). According to the teachings of Jesus, the man who lusts after a woman has broken the laws of

God that forbid adultery. The man who does this is a sinner and a lawbreaker.

Mohammed had a very different view of lust. When Mohammed saw Zaynab improperly dressed in her own home, he declared, "Praise be to Allah, who turns the hearts of men!" In other words, Allah was the one who caused Mohammed to desire Zaynab.

Therefore, lust was not necessarily something for which a man needed to repent. Lust might even come from Allah, who puts the desires in a man's heart. According to the revelations of Mohammed, this is what happened in the case of Zaynab.

There are a number of hadiths that indicate that Allah is the one who puts lust and adultery in the heart of a man. Consider the following hadiths:

> Narrated Ibn 'Abbas: I did not see anything so resembling minor sins as what Abu Huraira said from the Prophet, who said, "Allah has written for the son of Adam his inevitable share of adultery whether he is aware of it or not: The adultery of the eye is the looking (at something which is sinful to look at), and the adultery of the tongue is to utter (what it is unlawful to utter), and the innerself wishes and longs for (adultery) and the private parts turn that into reality or refrain from submitting to the temptation" (Bukhari 8:609).

> Abu Huraira reported Allah's Apostle as saying: Verily Allah has fixed the very portion of adultery which a man will indulge in, and which he of necessity must commit (Muslim 33:642).

> Allah fixed the very portion of adultery which a man will indulge in. There would be no escape from it (Muslim 33:6422).

In these hadiths it is clearly stated that Allah has decided how much adultery a man will commit. Who can oppose the will of God?

On another occasion, Mohammed evidently saw a woman and lusted after her. His solution for his lust can be found in the following hadiths. If a man feels lust for a woman who is not his wife, he should go to his wife and have sexual intercourse with her, so that the lust might go away.

> Jabir reported that Allah's Messenger saw a woman, and so he came to his wife, Zaynab, as she was tanning a leather and had sexual intercourse with her. He then went to his Companions and told them: The woman advances and retires in the shape of a devil, so when one

of you sees a woman, he should come to his wife, for that will repel what he feels in his heart (Muslim 8:3240).

Jabir heard Allah's Apostle say: When a woman fascinates any one of you and she captivates his heart, he should go to his wife and have an intercourse with her, for it would repel what he feels (Muslim 8:3242).

THE LAWS OF WAR

In the Law of Moses, there are laws that govern warfare. These laws are very different from the laws that apply in peacetime. For example, when a city was surrounded and placed under siege, if that city surrendered, the lives of its inhabitants would be spared, though they would be required to pay tribute to Israel. If that city did not surrender and the soldiers needed to attack over the walls of that city, the consequences were severe. Under the law of Moses, the men of that city could be killed and the women and children taken captive as servants (Deuteronomy 20:10-15).

These laws of warfare seem very harsh by modern standards. However, these are the laws of war that many civilizations have followed. When an army was required to attack over the walls of a besieged city, the consequences for that city were terrible. During the Middle Ages, both European armies and Muslim armies usually followed this law of war. If a besieged city surrendered, the men and women were usually allowed to live and tribute was paid. If a besieged city did not surrender, the men would be slaughtered, and the women and children taken as captives. One reason for this "law" is the fact that an army that must attack over the walls of a city is likely to lose many men. Therefore, an attacking army does everything in its power to pressure a besieged city to surrender.

Under the Law of Moses, there were certain laws that governed the treatment of a captive woman. If an Israelite warrior saw a captive woman whose husband had been killed in battle that he desired to have for himself, it was possible for him to marry that woman if he was willing to give her full rights as a wife. He was to bring her home and give her a full month to mourn the loss of her husband before marrying her. If he tired of her, he was not permitted to sell her as a slave. If he divorced her, she became a free woman. It was not permissible to rape captives, and then to sell them as slaves (Deuteronomy 21:10-14).

In some instances, Mohammed seemed to follow the Law of Moses. On certain occasions, when an enemy surrendered, they were allowed to keep their lives. Sometimes they were allowed to also keep their possessions, particularly if they converted to Islam. Sometimes they were slaughtered.

One big difference between Mohammed's behavior in wartime and the Law of Moses is the way that Mohammed's armies treated female prisoners. Quite simply, female prisoners often became sex slaves. They were raped, and then they were sold as slaves. Only occasionally were they married and given the full rights of wives as the Law of Moses required.

It is an undeniable fact that the soldiers of Mohammed were permitted to have sex with their captives. Sometimes a waiting period was followed and sometimes not.

This can be seen in the following hadith:

> Abu Sirma said to Abu Said al Khudri: "O Abu Said, did you hear Allah's messenger mentioning about al-azl (coitus interruptus)?" He said, "Yes", and added: "We went out with Allah's messenger on the expedition to the Mustaliq and took captive some excellent Arab women; and we desired them for we were suffering from the absence of our wives, (but at the same time) we also desired ransom for them. So we decided to have sexual intercourse with them but by observing azl (withdrawing the male sexual organ before emission of semen to avoid conception). But we said: 'We are doing an act whereas Allah's messenger is amongst us; why not ask him?' So we asked Allah's messenger and he said: 'It does not matter if you do not do it, for every soul that is to be born up to the Day of Resurrection will be born'" (Muslim 3371).

In this hadith, Mohammed's soldiers took captive some beautiful non-Muslim Arab women. They found themselves in a dilemma. They wanted to rape these women, but they also wanted to sell these women back to their families. If the women became pregnant, they would not be able to receive a high ransom for them from their families. Therefore, the Arab men wanted to practice "azl" (withdrawing the penis before semen was ejaculated) so that the women would not become pregnant. They went to Mohammed and asked his counsel. He told them to do whatever they wanted to do, that it would make no difference. If Allah wanted these women to become pregnant, they would become pregnant anyway.

A similar situation is recounted in the following hadith:

> Abu Said al-Khudri said: "The apostle of Allah sent a military expedition to Awtas on the occasion of the battle of Hunain. They met their enemy and fought with them. They defeated them and took them captives. Some of the Companions of the apostle of Allah were reluctant to have intercourse with the female captives in the presence of their husbands who were unbelievers. So Allah, the Exalted, sent down the Quranic verse, "And all married women (are forbidden) unto you save those (captives) whom your right hands possess". That is to say, they are lawful for them when they complete their waiting period" [The Quran verse is 4:24]. (Abu Dawud 2150).

On this occasion, Mohammed's men had taken both male and female captives. Once again they wanted to rape the female captives. However, they felt uncomfortable raping these women in front of their husbands. It just did n0t feel right to them to do this. So they decided to ask the counsel of Mohammed.

This time, Mohammed received a revelation from Allah that is written in the Quran: "And all married women (are forbidden) unto you save those (captives) whom your right hands possess" (Quran 4:24). In other words, a Muslim man was forbidden to sleep with a married woman, unless he possessed that woman as a captive or a slave. If that woman was his captive or his slave, he was free to rape her as long as he waited for the required period of time (usually until the woman had her period). It didn't matter if that woman's husband was still alive or not. He did not need to marry the woman. He could do as he liked with her.

It is very clear in the Quran that a man is allowed to have sex with his servants, captives, and slaves. Consider the following Quranic references:

> "...who restrain their carnal desires (except with their wives and slave girls, for these are lawful to them...)" (Quran - 23:5,6).

> "Prophet, We have made lawful to you the wives whom you have granted dowries and the slave girls whom God has given you as booty;.." (Quran - 33:50).

"...who restrain their carnal desires (except with their wives and slave girls, for these are lawful to them..." (QURAN - 23:5,6)

"Not so the worshippers, who are steadfast in prayer, who set aside a due portion of their wealth for the beggar and for the deprived, who truly believe in the Day of Reckoning and dread the punishment of their Lord (for none is secure from the punishment of their Lord); who restrain their carnal desire (save with their wives and their slave girls, for these are lawful to them: he that lusts after other than these is a transgressor..." (QURAN - 70:22-30).

The unrestrained rape of captives and slave girls that was practiced by Mohammed and his men would have been judged as adultery under the Law of Moses. Under the Law of Moses, a man was not permitted to have sex with women with whom he was not married. It did not matter if they were his captives or not.

Jesus taught a much higher standard than Moses. The Law of Moses permitted many things that were not permitted under the teachings of Jesus. When Jesus taught about the Law of Moses, he taught about the heart of God and the perfection of God. When Jesus taught about marriage, he taught about God's original purpose for marriage.

Jesus taught, "Have you not read that He who made them at the beginning 'made them male and female,' and said, 'For this reason a man shall leave his father and mother and be joined to his wife, and the two shall become one flesh' ? So then, they are no longer two but one flesh. Therefore what God has joined together, let not man separate" (Matthew 19:4-6).

If we study the Law of Moses as it was taught by Jesus, it seems that Mohammed broke this law. When Mohammed married the wife of his adopted son, he committed adultery according to the teachings of Jesus. When Mohammed lusted after a woman, he committed adultery according to the teachings of Jesus. And when Mohammed and his men raped their captives, they committed adultery according to the teachings of Jesus.

In each case, Mohammed received revelations from Allah that supported him in doing what he did. Allah revealed to Mohammed that Zaynab was to be his wife. Allah "turned the heart" of Mohammed towards Zaynab so that he desired her. Allah determined the amount of adultery that a man participated in. Allah revealed that a man was free to have sex with all women "whom his right hand possessed."

14 Neighbors

As we study the Ten Commandments of the Law of Moses, it is clear that these commandments fall into three categories. The first four commandments have to do with man's relationship to God:

1) You shall have no other gods before me.
2) You shall not make for yourself an idol to worship
3) You shall not take the name of the Lord your God in vain.
4) Remember the Sabbath day to keep it holy.

The fifth commandment deals with a man's relationship with his parents:

5) Honor your father and mother, that your days may be long.

The final five commandments are written this way:

6) You shall not murder.
7) You shall not commit adultery.
8) You shall not steal.
9) You shall not bear false witness against your neighbor.
10) You shall not covet your neighbor's house; you shall not covet your neighbor's wife, nor his male servant, nor his female servant, nor his ox, nor his donkey, nor anything that is your neighbor's.

There are some other verses in the Law of Moses that help us to better understand these last five commandments:

If a man acts with premeditation against his neighbor, to kill him by treachery, you shall take him from My altar, that he may die (Exodus 21:14).

You shall not lie carnally with your neighbor's wife, to defile yourself with her (Leviticus 18:20).

You shall not cheat your neighbor, nor rob him (Leviticus 19:13).

It is clear that these five commandments deal with a person's relationships to his neighbors. Under the law of God written by Moses, a person must not murder his neighbor, or commit adultery with his neighbor's wife, or steal from his neighbor, or lie to his neighbor, or covet his neighbor's house, wife, or possessions.

These teachings are summed up in Leviticus 19:18 where Moses writes the word of God, "You shall love your neighbor as yourself." Obviously, a person who loves his neighbor as himself will not murder his neighbor or steal his possessions. If he loves his neighbor, he will not lie to his neighbor or commit adultery with his neighbor's wife. Neither will he covet his neighbor's possessions. He will be happy when his neighbor is blessed instead of feeling jealous because of his neighbor's success.

According to the Law of Moses, these commandments applied to neighbors, not to the nation's enemies during wartime. When the children of Israel entered battle, they killed their enemies and plundered their goods. When they did these things under the command of God, they were not breaking the Law of Moses because these commandments apply to neighbors, not to enemies.

WHO IS MY NEIGHBOR?

One day as Jesus was teaching, a certain lawyer was listening to him. As he listened to Jesus teach about the kingdom of heaven, the lawyer began to feel very insecure. The level of righteousness that God required for His people was so high, that the lawyer began to doubt whether or not God would accept him into His kingdom. As his fears increased, he jumped to his feet and asked Jesus, "Teacher, what shall I do to inherit eternal life?"

Jesus responded by asking the man, "What is written in the Law of Moses? What is your reading of it?" Jesus wanted the man to understand not only the commandments of the Law of Moses, but the heart of God that was revealed in the Law of Moses. He wanted the man to tell him the most important points that were written in that law.

The lawyer answered Jesus, "'You shall love the LORD your God with all your heart, with all your soul, with all your strength, and with all your mind,' and 'you shall love your neighbor as yourself.'"

Jesus answered, "You have answered rightly; do this and you will live."

The lawyer understood that if he truly loved God, he would never break the first four commandments of the Law of Moses that deal with our relationship with God. He also understood that if he truly loved his neighbors, he would not break the final five commandments of the law. If he truly loved God and his neighbors, he would be able to keep the Law of Moses and not break it. The key to keeping the Law of Moses was to love God and to love one's neighbors.

But something troubled the lawyer. He understood that the key to keeping the Law of Moses was love: love for God, and love for one's neighbor. He knew that this love was actually necessary to enter heaven. One question troubled him. Whom must he love? Who was his neighbor?

And the man asked Jesus, "Who is my neighbor?"

This is a very important question. The answer to this question will reveal the one who keeps the law and the one who is a law-breaker.

Jesus responded by telling a story of two men. One was a Jew and the other a Samaritan. In those days, Jews and Samaritans hated one another. They both believed in one God, but their religions were very different from each other. The Jews followed the teachings of Moses and other prophets. They believed in one God and hated idolatry. The Samaritans also believed in God, but they were involved in many religious practices that were idolatrous. They worshiped God according to their traditions on the mountains. Sometimes they worshiped God, and sometimes they worshiped idols. They were a confused people. The Jews detested the Samaritans because they mixed idolatry with the true worship of God.

In Hfis story, the Jew was traveling from Jerusalem to Jericho, when he was attacked by robbers who beat him, stripped him, stole his possessions, and left him half dead by the side of the road. As he lay there gasping for breath, a Jewish priest passed by him. The priest ignored the suffering man and passed by on the other side of the road. Then another religious man, a Levite, also walked by. When he saw the suffering man, he moved to the other side of the road and kept walking.

Finally, a Samaritan came. He was a man of a different nation and a different religion. The Samaritan saw the Jew suffering by the side of the road, and he had compassion on him. He went to the man and poured oil and wine on his wounds and wrapped them in bandages. He put the man on his donkey, and took him to an inn where he took care of him. The next day when he departed, he paid the innkeeper enough money to continue caring for the man.

After telling the story, Jesus asked the lawyer, "Which of these three men do you think was a neighbor to him who was attacked by the thieves?" The lawyer answered, "He who showed mercy on him." Jesus said, "Go and do likewise" (Luke 10).

This is extremely important. The Law of Moses clearly shows that the last five commandments of the Law of Moses apply to our neighbors. In this parable, Jesus tells us who our neighbors are. The Jews and Samaritans were from different tribes and different religions. And yet Jesus taught that they were neighbors.

If Jews and Samaritans were supposed to treat each other as neighbors, then a man's neighbors include those who are from different tribes and different religions. The Samaritans did not have the correct religion. Sometimes they even worshipped idols. It seemed that the Jews had good reasons to hate the Samaritans. And yet Jesus taught that Jews and Samaritans needed to treat one another as neighbors if they hoped to keep the Law of Moses and enter the kingdom of heaven.

This is extremely important. Jesus taught that it is not only important to treat your friends well. Even idol worshipers treat their friends well. It is not enough just to love those who love you. Even idol worshipers love those who love them. Jesus taught that the love that is truly righteous in God's eyes is a love so strong that a man will love his neighbor as himself.

How do you treat your neighbors? They might not share the same religion as you do. They might come from a different ethnic background. They might look different and understand things differently. They are not your brothers, who share the same family and religion with you. They are your neighbors, and the differences between you may be great. Yet the way you treat them will determine whether or not you have kept the Law or broken the Law, because the Law of Moses focuses on a man's relationship with his neighbors.

15 You Shall Not Steal

Moses taught his followers, "You shall not steal." Jesus also taught his followers not to steal, but he went much further in this teaching than Moses did. Jesus wanted his followers to have hearts full of the love of God, instead of the love of money. Jesus taught his followers to leave everything and to follow him. He taught them not to worry about money or to love money, because they have a Father in heaven who takes care of them. Jesus taught his followers to store up for themselves treasures in heaven, instead of storing up treasure on earth.

Jesus taught his followers to be generous and to give to those who needed help. He taught his followers not only to help their friends and family but also to help their neighbors. He taught that a man's neighbors included those who came from a different nation and a different religion.

The Quran teaches Muslims that they should not steal from other Muslims. The punishment for theft is severe in the Quran. It is written in the Quran,

> As to the thief, male or female, cut off his or her hands: a punishment by way of example, from Allah, for their crime: and Allah is Exalted in power (Quran 5:38).

However, the laws of God do not only apply to those who have the same religion that you have. The Law of Moses applies to one's neighbors. When

Mohammed and the Muslims were based in Medina, they had neighbors. Their neighbors were the three Jewish tribes of Medina, the Banu Qaynuqa, the Banu Nadir, and the Banu Qurayza.

When Mohammed and his followers were chased out of Mecca in 622 by pagan Arabs who did not want to receive his revelations or his religion, the three Jewish tribes of Medina welcomed him to their city. These tribes had been disputing among themselves and with the Arabs for many years. They invited Mohammed to come to their town to act as a mediator, a peacemaker among the tribes. They made a covenant of peace with Mohammed, and formed the Charter of Medina which stipulated how the city would be ruled.

Surely these Jewish tribes were Mohammed's neighbors. According to the Law of Moses, Mohammed could not steal from them or abuse them in any way. According to the Law of Moses and the teachings of Jesus, Mohammed should have loved his neighbors as he loved himself. He should have treated the Jewish tribes of Medina as he wanted to be treated. And yet as Mohammed and the Muslims increased in power, their Jewish neighbors lost everything.

One day after leaving the mosque in Medina, Mohammed called his men and said, "Let us go to the Jews." The Muslims approached the Jews, and Mohammed declared to them, "If you embrace Islam, you will be safe. You should know that the earth belongs to Allah and His Apostle, and I want to expel you from this land. So, if anyone amongst you owns some property, he is permitted to sell it, otherwise you should know that the Earth belongs to Allah and his apostle" (Bukhari 4:392).

So, just a short time after the Jews invited Mohammed to come to Medina as a mediator and a peacemaker, Mohammed declared that the entire earth belonged to him, including all the land of the Jews. He declared the way in which he intended to treat his neighbors. He intended to expel them from Medina and take their land.

Mohammed carried through on his promise. Within less than two years after Mohammed arrived in Medina, two of those tribes, the Banu Qaynuqa and the Banu Nadir were evicted from Medina by the Muslims. Their Muslim neighbors took their lands and their wealth, allowing them only to escape with what they could carry on their backs and camels. The fate of the final tribe, the Banu Qurayza, was much worse.

BANU QAYNUQA

The first tribe to be expelled was the Banu Qaynuqa. Mohammed knew that this tribe was the easiest target. The other two Jewish tribes were unlikely to support the Banu Qaynuqa because both tribes had recently been involved in a conflict with this tribe.

A Jewish man from the Banu Qaynuqa insulted a Muslim woman by lifting her dress, and in the chaos that followed she was stripped naked. A Muslim man killed the Jew who was responsible. Then an angry mob of Jews from the Banu Qaynuqa tribe killed the Muslim man in retaliation. Mohammed used this event as an excuse to attack the entire Banu Qaynuqa community.

Mohammed and his men launched an attack against the Banu Qaynuqa. The Banu Qaynuqa had only about 700 fighting men, and they retreated to their fortress where Mohammed's men put them under siege for fourteen days. After fourteen days, they surrendered.

Mohammed bound the hands of his captives. He wanted to execute the men of the tribe, but an Arab man named Abdullah pleaded for the lives of the Jews, saying, "O Mohammed, deal kindly with my clients." Mohammed became angry, but Abdullah refused to give up. He thrust his hand into the prophet's robe, holding on to Mohammed until he relented. Finally, Mohammed said, "You can have them," and the lives of the Jews were spared. The Jews were exiled from Medina with the few things they were able to carry. Everything else was divided up among the Muslims. Mohammed took one fifth of their possessions as his personal share of the loot.

And so the covenant between Mohammed and the Jews of Banu Qaynuqa was broken. Mohammed received a revelation that it was okay to break a covenant if he feared that his covenant partner was treacherous. It is written in the Quran:

> If thou fearest treachery from any group, throw back (their covenant) to them, (so as to be) on equal terms: for Allah loveth not the treacherous (Quran 8:58).

Mohammed also received a revelation that affect one's neighbors. Muslims are not supposed to have close friends who are not Muslims. It is written in the Quran:

121

"O you who believe! Do not take for intimate friends from among others than your own people; they do not fall short of inflicting loss upon you; they love what distresses you; vehement hatred has already appeared from out of their mouths, and what their breasts conceal is greater still; indeed, We have made the communications clear to you, if you will understand (Quran 3:118).

BANU NADIR

In the case of the second Jewish tribe, the Banu Nadir, the reason for their banishment seems almost trivial. One of Mohammed's soldiers murdered two members of an Arab tribe that had a covenant with Mohammed. In order to keep peace with that tribe, Mohammed agreed to pay blood money to the offended tribe. Instead of asking the Muslims to pay all of the blood money, he demanded the Jews of the Banu Nadir pay a portion of the blood money, even though they were not involved at all in the murders.

Naturally, the Jews balked at this request. They met with one another as they discussed Mohammed's demand. Some were in favor of giving Mohammed what he wanted, while others disagreed. The Jews delayed their payment until late in the day, as Mohammed waited outside their homes.

While he was waiting, Mohammed received the revelation that the Jews were planning to assassinate him by dropping a stone on his head (Ibn Ishaq). He left the Jewish settlement and returned with his army. They surrounded the Jews and placed the community under siege for 14 days.

In the end, the Jews of Banu Nadir surrendered without a fight. Mohammed allowed them to leave Medina with what they and their camels could carry. They left in a great caravan of 600 camels. The women were dressed in their finest apparel, and the music of pipes and tambourines was played as they paraded through the streets of Medina saying their final farewell to their home.

Mohammed received a revelation from Allah concerning his victory over the Banu Nadir. It is written in the Quran:

Quran 59:0-7, Rashad

(59) In the name of God, Most Gracious, Most Merciful

(59:1) Glorifying GOD is everything in the heavens and the earth, and He is the Almighty, Most Wise.

(59:2) He is the One who evicted those who disbelieved among the people of the scripture from their homes in a mass exodus. You never thought that they would leave, and they thought that their preparations would protect them from GOD. But then GOD came to them whence they never expected, and threw terror into their hearts. Thus, they abandoned their homes on their own volition, in addition to pressure from the believers. You should learn from this, O you who possess vision.

(59:3) If GOD did not force them to leave, He would have requited them in this life (even worse than forcing them to leave). In the Hereafter He will commit them to the retribution of Hell.

(59:4) This is because they opposed GOD and His messenger. For those who oppose GOD and His messenger, GOD is most strict in enforcing retribution.

(59:5) Whether you chop a tree, or leave it standing on its trunk, is in accordance with GOD's will. He will surely humiliate the wicked.

(59:6) Whatever GOD restored for His messenger was not the result of your war efforts, whether you fought on horses or on foot. GOD is the One who sends His messengers against whomever He wills. GOD is Omnipotent.

(59:7) Whatever GOD restored to His messenger from the (defeated) communities shall go to GOD and His messenger (in the form of a charity). You shall give it to the relatives, the orphans, the poor, and the traveling alien. Thus, it will not remain monopolized by the strong among you. You may keep the spoils given to you by the messenger, but do not take what he enjoins you from taking. You shall reverence GOD. GOD is strict in enforcing retribution.

The Law of Moses did not permit the Israelites to destroy the food-producing trees of a city that they besieged.   The Law of Moses states, "When you besiege a city for a long time, while making war against it to take it, you shall not destroy its trees by wielding an ax against them; if you can eat of them, do not cut them down to use in the siege, for the tree of the field is man's food."

During the siege of the Banu Nadir, Mohammed ordered the valuable date-palm trees of the Banu Nadir to be chopped down and burned. He received a revelation from Allah that it was ok for him to do this. This is what verse five (above) is referring to: "Whether you chop a tree, or leave it standing on its trunk, is in accordance with GOD's will. He will surely humiliate the wicked."

Mohammed himself took possession of the lands, houses, weapons and remaining possessions of the Banu Nadir. He received the revelation that he did not need to share most of the booty with his warriors because not much fighting was involved. Verses six and seven quoted above support Mohammed's decision to not give his soldiers their normal share of the booty. Instead, Mohammed divided much of this wealth among the Meccans who had emigrated with him to Medina. He used the rest of this wealth to support his family and to buy horses and weapons for future fights (Bukhari 4:153).

The Banu Nadir left Medina. Most of them emigrated to the nearby city of Khaybar. It would have been better for them had they placed a greater distance between themselves and Mohammed.

The third Jewish tribe of Medina was the Banu Qurayza. We will discuss the fate of this tribe in the following chapter.

KHAYBAR

The refugees from Banu Nadir settled in Khaybar. Khaybar was an oasis located about 100 miles north of Medina. The Jews of Khaybar formed a prosperous community there, growing date-palms and engaging in business.

Meanwhile, Mohammed faced some challenges from the pagan Arabs of Mecca. In 628, after a failed pilgrimage to Mecca, Mohammed and the Muslims entered into a peace treaty with the Meccans, the treaty of Hudaybiyyah. This treaty seemed humiliating to some of the Muslims. In the treaty, the Meccans refused to recognize the prophethood of Mohammed. The Muslims were forbidden to enter Mecca that year but could enter the following year instead.

As the Muslims left Mecca, Mohammed received a revelation through his angel that should have encouraged the people: "We have given you a glorious victory so that God may forgive you your past and future sins" (Quran 48:1). In spite of this revelation, some of the Muslims grumbled about the situation. It did not seem like a victory, whether their sins were forgiven or not. It seemed that the Meccans had received the better part of the deal, that the Meccans were the stronger party in the negotiations.

Six weeks later, Mohammed led his men on a military mission to prove that God was indeed giving them victory. He led his men on an attack against his neighbors, the Jews of Khaybar.

Some Muslim historians have tried to make the claim that these Jews were at war with Mohammed. In fact, the testimony from the hadiths show that they were not at war. As Mohammed and his army marched towards Khaybar, he gave a command to his nephew Ali: "Proceed on and do not look about until Allah grants you victory!"

Ali proceeded for a while, and then he turned around and spoke in a loud voice, "Allah's Messenger, on what issue should I fight with the people?"

Mohammed answered, "Fight with them until they bear testimony to the fact that there is no god but Allah and Mohammed is his messenger" (Muslim 5917).

This passage makes it clear that Mohammed's men did not know why they were attacking the Jews of Khaybar. There was no war taking place. The Khaybar were not a threat to the Muslims. The attack on the Khaybar was not taking place out of necessity. The only justification for attacking Khaybar was that the Jews there did not recognize Mohammed as a true prophet.

The morning of the attack, as Mohammed and his men approached Khaybar, they did not meet soldiers. Instead they met farm workers coming to work in their fields, carrying their spades and buckets. When they saw Mohammed and his army they cried, "Mohammed and his force!" as they turned and fled back to the city. The Jews were caught completely by surprise. Until the attack came, they did not even realize that they were at war.

And so the battle began. Mohammed's men moved quickly to conquer the unprepared city. They moved from farm to farm and then from fort to fort.

The forts fell one by one. At the citadel of Qamus, a Jewish warrior and chieftain named Marhab left the forts and engaged Ali in single combat, who slayed him.

The last two forts to be attacked were Al-Watih and Al-Sulalim, which were besieged for ten nights. Finally the Jews surrendered. They agreed to leave the area and to surrender their wealth to the Muslims.

The Jewish women were taken captive as sex-slaves. They were bound with ropes and distributed to the Muslim warriors as booty. One of these captives was Safiyya bint Huyayy, the daughter of a Jewish chief. Safiyya was a beautiful woman, and the men brought word of her to Mohammed who decided to take her as his wife.

Safiyya's husband was a man named Kenana ibn Al-Rabi. He was a member of the Banu Nadir tribe that had fled from Medina to Khaybar. It was rumored that Kenana had hidden treasure somewhere in the conquered city. Mohammed ordered his men to torture Kenana until he disclosed the location of the treasure. A fire was kindled with flint and steel on the man's chest. In extreme pain, Kenana told the men where the treasure was hidden. Mohamed's men found the treasure, and then they beheaded Kenana.

Mohammed's men killed Safiyya's father, husband, and brother. After the killing was finished, Mohammed planned his wedding with Safiyya. Although the Quran instructs a widow to wait four months and ten days before marrying a new husband, Mohammed married Safiyya only a few days after the battle of Khaybar (Quran 2:234-235). Today, the members of ISIS follow Mohammed's example as they distribute female captives among themselves to be raped soon after a battle is finished.

Some of the surviving Jews approached Mohammed and requested that they might remain on their lands and continue cultivating their orchards. They offered Mohammed one half of their produce in return. Mohammed agreed, on the condition that the Muslims could expel the Jews at any time they wished (Ibn Hisham).

Moses taught that a man should not steal from his neighbor, or covet his neighbor's possessions, or commit adultery with his neighbor's wife. At Khaybar Mohammed did all these things and worse. He stole his neighbor's goods. He tortured and murdered them. He and his men took their wives and daughters and raped them.

THE RAIDS OF MOHAMMED

During the last ten years of Mohammed's life, from 622 AD until 632 AD, Mohammed and his followers were involved in almost constant warfare against their neighbors and their enemies. Mohammed launched 100 raids, expeditions, and invasions against his neighbors and enemies. He personally took part in 27 of these battles.

One of the primary reasons for these raids and expeditions was booty. Mohammed and his men were raiders. They lived by stealing.

In the beginning, most of the raids were launched against the Meccans who had driven Mohammed out of their city to Medina. Mohammed's men raided the caravans of the Meccans, seizing their trade goods. Whenever possible, they captured women and used them as sex-slaves until they could be sold for ransom back to the Meccans. When the Meccan army came out to protect the caravans, the battle of Badr was fought, in which the Muslims won their first major victory.

One such raid against an Arab tribe known as the Bani Mustaliq is described in the hadiths:

> "The Prophet had suddenly attacked Bani Mustaliq without warning while they were heedless and their cattle were being watered at the places of water. Their fighting men were killed, and their women and children were taken as captives" (Bukhari 3:717).

When it was necessary, Mohammed received revelations justifying the stealing. He received the revelation that the Banu Nadir wanted to assassinate him, justifying his theft of all their possessions. He received the revelation that the whole earth belonged to him and Allah, justifying his theft of the possessions of the Banu Qaynuqa. The revelations that Mohammed received from his angel always supported the actions that he took.

Here are some verses of the Quran that support the stealing done by Mohammed:

> GOD has promised you many spoils that you will gain. He thus advanced some benefits for you in this life, and He has withheld the

people's hands of aggression against you, and has rendered this a sign for the believers. He thus guides you in a straight path (Quran 48:20).

"So enjoy what you took as booty; the spoils are lawful and good" (Quran 8:69).

Mohammed believed that of all the prophets, he alone was allowed to steal. Mohammed received a revelation in which certain things were given to him that were given to no other prophet who came before him.

Narrated Jabir bin 'Abdullah:

The Prophet said, "I have been given five things which were not given to anyone else before me.

1. Allah made me victorious by awe, (by His frightening my enemies) for a distance of one month's journey.

2. The earth has been made for me (and for my followers) a place for praying and a thing to perform Tayammum, therefore, anyone of my followers can pray wherever the time of a prayer is due.

3. The booty has been made Halal (lawful) for me yet it was not lawful for anyone else before me.

4. I have been given the right of intercession (on the Day of Resurrection).

5. Every Prophet used to be sent to his nation only but I have been sent to all mankind (Bukhari 1:331).

The third thing given to Mohammed was booty: "The booty has been made Halal (lawful) for me yet it was not lawful for anyone else before me." In other words, it was lawful for Mohammed to steal, although no prophet before him had been allowed to steal. When you combine these words with Mohammed's declaration that the whole earth belonged to Allah and His apostle, the result is easy to predict.

The result is a prophet who believes that he can take anything he wants. Unlike other robbers and thieves, this prophet is not ashamed of his sin. He does not hide his sin. He proudly declares that it was God who gives him ownership of all things and the right to steal all things.

Unfortunately for Mohammed, the righteousness of God does not change. Moses declared, "You shall not steal." Jesus also taught on this subject, and he revealed the heart of God and the righteousness of God on a much higher level than Moses did. When Mohammed stands before God, he will be judged by the Law of Moses and the teachings of Jesus. When he stands before God, he will stand as one who stole everything he was able to steal from his neighbors, while declaring that it was God's will for him to do so.

Vaughn Martin

16 You Shall Not Murder

The Law of Moses commands us not to murder. Under the Law of Moses, the penalty for murder was death. When Jesus taught from the Law of Moses, he taught that murder begins in a man's heart. The man who hates his brother in his heart is guilty in the eyes of God.

Laws of warfare are also discussed in the Law of Moses. The Law of Moses states what must happen when an enemy city surrenders (Deuteronomy 20). Jesus did not teach about how to properly engage in warfare, because Jesus never sent his servants with swords to fight. Jesus did not establish an earthly kingdom with the swords of men. Jesus taught of a heavenly kingdom that must be established in men's hearts before it is established over the nations.

God has promised that those who commit bloodshed will be judged, both in this world and in the age to come. The nation that loves to shed blood will suffer in warfare. It is written in the Torah, "Whoever sheds the blood of man, by man his blood will be shed" (Genesis 9:6). Jesus said, "Those who live by the sword will die by the sword"(Matt.26:52). On judgment day, murderers will be cast into the lake of fire with idolaters, adulterers and unbelievers.

But the cowardly, unbelieving, abominable, murderers, sexually immoral, sorcerers, idolaters, and all liars shall have their part in the lake which burns with fire and brimstone, which is the second death (Revelation 21:8).

THE FATE OF THE BANU QURAYZA

The Law of Moses is very focused on the way that one should treat his neighbor. When Mohammed was based in Medina his neighbors were the three Jewish tribes of Medina. We have already discussed what happened to the Banu Qaynuqa and the Banu Nadir. Now we must look at what happened to the third tribe, the Banu Qurayza.

Even while Mohammed made war against the first two tribes, he made a treaty with the Banu Qurayza (Abu Dawud 3004). It is not possible to know the exact terms of this treaty. Some scholars claim that the treaty required the Banu Qurayza to join Mohammed in battle against his enemies, while others claim that the treaty simply required the Banu Qurayza to refrain from aiding the enemies of Mohammed.

In 627 AD, Abu Sufyan led the Arabs of Mecca on an attack against the Muslims based in Medina that became known as the "Battle of the Trench." In this battle, about 3,000 Muslim warriors faced a much larger force of invaders mounted on horses. Mohammed and his men dug trenches on the northern side of their position that the horses of the invaders were not able to cross.

The result was a stalemate. For 27 days the invaders laid siege to the Muslim positions. Finally, as the weather worsened, they retreated with very few casualties on either side. Only three invaders were killed and six Muslims.

After the battle, Mohammed was not satisfied with the actions of his "allies," the Jews of the Banu Qurayza tribe. The Jewish tribe was positioned to the south of Mohammed's forces. Although they supplied the Muslim forces with spades, picks, and baskets to dig the trench that helped the Muslims win the battle (Al-Waqidi), they did not get involved in the actual fighting with the invading Meccans. Rumors and accusations began to circulate that the Jews had entered into secret negotiations with the Meccans against Mohammed.

It has not been proven that the Banu Qurayza made any kind of agreement with the invading Meccans. There is actually no hadith that indicates that the

Banu Qurayza renounced their treaty with Mohammed, although many modern Islamic scholars claim that they did. There is one hadith that states that Abu Sufyan (the leader of the Meccans) was turned down by the Banu Qurayza when he sought their help against Mohammed. It states that the Banu Qurayza refused to let the Meccans cross their territory to attack the Muslims from the south during the battle.

> So Abu Sufyan said, "O ye people of Quraysh, by Allah your [current] dwelling is not a place to be dwelled in [meaning that their current situation is bad]; the horses [and camels, mules, etc..] have died, **Bani Quraytha has turned us down - we received from them what we don't like [meaning they refused to let them in through their fortresses]**, and this wind is giving us what you see [a hard time]. By Allah, our cauldrons aren't standing, the fires aren't lasting, and the structures aren't holding. So retreat for I am retreating" (Musnad Ahmad <u>2283</u>).

In any case, the Jews did not take up arms against Mohammed. They did not attack Mohammed's forces, or kill any Muslims. The above hadith indicates that they might have helped Mohammed by not allowing the Meccans to attack the Muslims from the south. It is possible that they remained as neutral as possible in the battle, waiting to see the outcome before strongly taking sides.

The following hadith narrates what took place when Mohammed met the angel Gabriel after he returned from the Battle of the Trench:

> Narrated 'Aisha:
> When Allah's Apostle returned on the day (of the battle) of Al-Khandaq (i.e. Trench), he put down his arms and took a bath. Then Gabriel whose head was covered with dust, came to him saying, "You have put down your arms! By Allah, I have not put down my arms yet." Allah's Apostle said, "Where (to go now)?" Gabriel said, "This way," pointing towards the tribe of Banu Qurayza. So Allah's Apostle went out towards them (Bukhari 4:68).

FIGHTING THE QURAYZA

And so after the Battle of the Trench was over, the angel Gabriel sent Mohammed to fight his allies, the Jews of the Banu Qurayza, who had never attacked him. Mohammed's 3,000 fighting men far outnumbered the men of Banu Qurayza. As his soldiers advanced, the Jews retreated to their stronghold, where Mohammed's men placed them under siege for 25 days.

As the siege dragged on, the Jews became desperate. They offered to surrender to Mohammed and leave their land and property if Mohammed would allow them to take one camel load of possessions per person. When this request was refused, they offered to surrender if Mohammed would allow them to depart without any property. This request was also refused.

As the Jews became desperate, they discussed different options among themselves such as embracing Islam or making a desperate surprise attack on the Muslims. At one point they asked to negotiate with a former Arab ally who was with Mohammed's forces, Abu Lubaba. Abu Lubaba was a member of the Aws tribe, which was a former ally of the Jews. In the meeting, Abu Lubaba advised the Jews to surrender, but he also gave them a clear warning of what would happen if they surrendered. He made a sign with his hand toward his throat, indicating that there would be a slaughter (Ibn Ishaq p. 462).

In spite of this warning, the Jews finally decided to surrender unconditionally to Mohammed and to place their future in his hands. The hands of the men were tied behind their backs, and they were marched to the city of Medina. Some of the former Arab allies of the Jews asked for leniency from Mohammed, but their request was denied.

Mohammed chose a judge who would decide the fate of the Jews, Sa'd ibin Mu'adh. The Jews had little choice but to accept Mohammed's choice. Sa'd was a leader of the Aws tribe, the former ally of the Jews, so it might have been thought that he would have some sympathy for the Jews.

However, Mohammed knew Sa'd well. Sa'd was a hot-tempered man who believed that infidels should be slaughtered. Sa'd was Mohammed's personal bodyguard in the battle of Badr. In that battle, Sa'd seemed displeased when he saw that the Arab prisoners captured by Mohammed's men were allowed to live. When Mohammed saw Sa'd's response, he asked him if he was displeased. Sa'd answered, "Yes, by God. It is the first defeat that God has brought on the infidel and I would rather see them slaughtered than left alive" (Sirat p. 301).

During the battle of the Trench, Sa'd was struck in his arm by an arrow shot by the Meccans. The wound became infected. During the days that followed, Mohammed pitched a tent for Sa'd right in the mosque so that he could easily visit with Sa'd during his recuperation. Sa'd's condition worsened. When Mohammed appointed Sa'd as judge over the Jews, it was clear that Sa'd was dying from his wound.

It is very likely that Mohammed knew exactly what Sa'd's judgment would be. Mohammed had spent time visiting with Sa'd on his deathbed. He knew Sa'd's temperament and what Sa'd had declared on similar occasions.

Sa'd gave his verdict for the Jews of the Banu Qurayza: ""I give my judgment that their warriors should be killed, their women and children should be taken as captives, and their properties distributed" (Bukhari 5:448).

Mohammed supported Sa'd's decision with the words: "O Sa'd! You have judged amongst them with (or similar to) the judgment of the King Allah" (Bukhari, 4:280 see also 5:148, 8:278).

THE END OF THE BANU QURAYZA

Immediately following this judgment, the men of the Banu Qurayza were led to the market of Medina. They were between 600 to 900 in number. Trenches were dug, and all the men were beheaded. Their headless bodies were buried in the trenches. Mohammed watched over the entire proceeding.

One woman began to lose her mind as she watched the slaughter. She began to laugh uncontrollably in a bizarre manner. A Muslim man took her and beheaded her (Abu Dawud 14:2665).

The rest of the women were distributed among the Muslim warriors as sex slaves, and the children were also distributed as slaves. The bodies of the young men were inspected. If they were old enough to grow pubic hair, they were executed. Otherwise they became slaves. Mohammed chose one woman named Rayhana for himself. All the property of the Jews was divided up among the Muslims, and Mohammed took his usual share of 20 percent.

In this way the tribe of the Banu Qurayza came to its end. They were slaughtered by their neighbors. The only justification for this slaughter comes from the revelations received by Mohammed.

Some Muslims have tried to justify Mohammed's actions by claiming that he acted in obedience to Deuteronomy 20: 9-13 which told the Jews to kill the male inhabitants of a city that did not agree to surrender. Of course, the Jews of Banu Qurayza did surrender. According to the Law of Moses, they should have been shown mercy.

According to the Law of Moses, Mohammed committed murder when he ordered the Jews of the Banu Qurayza to be executed. These Jews never attacked Mohammed. The soldiers of Mohammed did not suffer any losses at the hands of the Jews of the Banu Qurayza. The soldiers of Mohammed did not need to launch an attack over the walls of the fortress of the Banu Qurayza. The only thing that justified the killing of the Banu Qurayza was the revelation of Mohammed.

If Mohammed is to be judged by the standard of Jesus, then there is no question about the outcome. According to the teachings of Jesus, the Banu Qurayza were the neighbors of Mohammed. They should have been treated in the way that Mohammed would have wanted to be treated. Instead, they were murdered. Mohammed demonstrated deep hatred of his neighbors as he agreed that they should be slaughtered.

Jesus taught that if a man hopes to be forgiven by God for his sins, he must also forgive those who sinned against him: **"For if you forgive men their trespasses, your heavenly Father will also forgive you. But if you do not forgive men their trespasses, neither will your Father forgive your trespasses" (Matthew 6:14-15).**

Even if it was true that the Banu Qurayza broke their treaty with Mohammed, the man who hopes to be forgiven by God must also forgive. If Mohammed could not forgive the Banu Qurayza for their failures, can Mohammed expect to be forgiven by God for his failures?

When you study the life of Mohammed, you will read of many times when Mohammed refused to forgive his enemies or show them any mercy at all. Frequently, the sins of Mohammed's enemies seem to be very minor indeed. The three Jewish tribes of Medina did very, very little to harm Mohammed in any way, and yet they lost everything, including their lives. If you were not a follower of Mohammed, you could expect no mercy from him at all.

MOHAMMED AND THE POETS

Mohammed hired poets to mock his enemies. When he and his men laid siege to the Banu Qurayza, he hired a poet named Hassan and said to him, "Abuse them (with your poems), and Gabriel is with you (i.e., supports you)" (Bukhari 5:449).

Although Mohammed hired poets of his own, he showed very little tolerance for those who wrote mocking poems about him. Mohammed frequently ordered the death of men and women who mocked or criticized him with songs and poetry.

There were two slave girls in Mecca who used to sing songs and recite poems that mocked Mohammed. When Mohammed entered Mecca with his army in 629 AD, his soldiers were not permitted to slaughter civilians--with a few exceptions. Mohammed said, "There are four persons whom I shall not give protection" (Abu Dawud 14:2678). These four people included two girls who used to sing songs mocking the prophet. One of them, Fartana, was killed by Mohammed's soldiers, while the other one converted to Islam.

A BLIND MAN MURDERS HIS WIFE

In another instance, there was a blind man who owned a female slave who was the mother of his children. This woman used to criticize and mock Mohammed. The blind man rebuked her and attempted to stop her criticisms and accusations, but she refused to stop. One night the blind man took a dagger and stabbed her in the belly. The blood of the woman covered her child who was clinging to her.

The next day, Mohammed was told what had happened. Mohammed assembled the people and demanded that the man who had killed the woman stand up. The blind man arose trembling and approached the prophet. He explained to Mohammed why he killed the woman. When Mohammed heard the explanation, he said, "Oh, be witness, no retaliation is payable for her blood" (Abu Dawud 38:4348, 38:4349, 38:4361).

With these words, the prophet made it clear that the murder of this woman was justified. The killer was not required to pay any blood money to the woman's relatives. He was not punished in any way.

THE MURDER OF KA'B

The first major victory of the Muslim army took place at the battle of Badr, in which the Muslim army defeated an army of Meccans who were trying to stop the Muslim raids on their caravans. This event took place before the time that Mohammed drove the Banu Nadir tribe of Jews out of Medina. There was a Jew of the Banu Nadir named Ka'b al-Ashraf. Ka'b was a friend of the Quraysh tribe of Mecca. He sympathized with the Meccans who were killed in the battle of Badr. He thought it was disgraceful that some Arab nobles had been slaughtered and thrown into a pit in the battle. After the battle, he moved to Mecca, where he wrote poetry mourning the Arabs who died in the battle of Badr. He criticized the prophet and wrote poetry mocking the Muslim women.

When Mohammed heard of Ka'b's mockery, he became furious. He said, "Who is willing to kill Ka`b bin al-Ashraf, who has hurt Allah and His apostle?"

A man named Maslama responded, "I will deal with him for you, O apostle of God. I will kill him."

He said, "Do so if you can." Maslama then asked for permission from Mohammed to deceive Ka'b so that he might be killed.

Maslama gathered four friends to help him deceive and murder Ka'b. One of the men named Silkan visited Ka'b at his home during the day and complained about the chaos that Mohammed was causing between the different Arab and Jewish tribes. He proposed a business deal between Ka'b and Maslama's associates. It was agreed that some weapons were to be a part of the deal.

And so Silkan called Maslama and the others to visit Ka'b. They came to his house by night, carrying the weapons that were supposed to be part of the business deal. They called Ka'b out of bed. He left his house, and they walked together. The men flattered Ka'b and gained his trust, until the cry rang out, "Smite the enemy of God!" The men drew their weapons, and Maslama stabbed Ka'b in the back with his dagger, throwing all his weight upon it until it reached his genitals. Ka'b fell to the ground, mortally wounded by Muslims who pretended to be his friends (Ibn Ishaq/Hisham 552).

THE MURDER OF ABU RAFI

The men who murdered Ka'b were members of the Aus tribe. At that time there were two Arab tribes among Mohammed's followers, the Aus and the Khazraj, that used to compete with each other to show how devoted they were to Mohammed. When the Khazraj heard what the Aus had done to Ka'b they said to one another, "They should not have superiority over us in the Apostle's eyes and in Islam" (Sirat, p. 714).

And so the Khazraj looked for a murder that they could commit that would put them on equal footing with the Aus. They remembered that there was a Jewish merchant in Khaybar named Abu Rafi, who had also criticized Mohammed. They came to Mohammed and asked for his permission to murder this man. Mohammed gave them his blessing.

And so a group of men from Khazraj set out on their mission. They came to the castle where Abu Rafi stayed. The gatekeeper was closing the gate for the evening. One of the men pretended to be one of the cattle herders from the castle, and he was able to enter before the gate closed. Once inside, he was able to obtain the keys to the gate.

When night fell, he silently opened the gate, and then went seeking Abu Rafi. He called out Abu Rafi's name, and when Abu Rafi responded, he approached him and stabbed him in the belly with his sword. Then he escaped through the open gate (Bukhari 4:264, 5:371, 5:372).

THE MURDER OF ABU AFAK

On another occasion, there was a Jew named Abu Afak who was upset because Mohammed had ordered the killing of a man named Al-Harith bin Suwayd for leaving Islam. Abu Afak expressed his unhappiness by writing a poem that was critical of Mohammed. When Mohammed heard about the poem, he said, "Who will deal with this rascal for me?"

Salim Ibn Umayr responded to the call. He knew that Abu Afak liked to sleep out in the open. He located the place where Abu Afak was sleeping and stabbed him in his sleep (The book of The Major Classes, Volume 2, (2), p.32 ibn Sa'd al-Baghdadi).

THE MURDER OF ASMA BINT MARWAN

Asma, the daughter of Marwan, was the mother of five children. Asma became deeply troubled by the killing of Abu Afak, and wrote a poem to the Muslims expressing her distress. She ridiculed the Arabs of Medina for accepting a leader who was not originally from Medina:

> You obey a stranger who is none of yours (Mohammed),
> One not of Murad or Madhhij
> Do you expect good from him after the killing of your chiefs?
> Is there no man of pride who would attack him by surprise
> And cut off the hopes of those who expect something from him?

When Mohammed heard about this poem, he said, 'Who will rid me of Marwan's daughter?"

Umayr bin Adiy al Khatmi answered the call. Umayr was a blind man who could find his way in the dark. He entered Asma's bedroom at night where she was sleeping with all her children, the youngest held close to her chest. Umayr carefully removed the child from her and killed her (Sirat p. 676).

THE SIN OF KUFR

If a Muslim makes a joke about Mohammed, the penalty for his joke is severe indeed. It was revealed to Mohammed that the man who mocks him is guilty of kufr (disbelief). In other words, the Muslim who mocks or criticizes Mohammed is guilty of kufr towards Allah. If he speaks idly or foolishly about Mohammed, he is guilty of kufr. The Muslim who does this can expect no mercy.

This revelation is found in the Quran:

Quran 9:64-66 (Rashad)

(9:64) The hypocrites worry that a sura may be revealed exposing what is inside their hearts. Say, "Go ahead and mock. God will expose exactly what you are afraid of."

(9:65) If you ask them, they would say, "We were only mocking and kidding." Say, "Do you realize that you are mocking God, and His revelations, and His messenger?"

(9:66) Do not apologize. You have disbelieved after having believed. If we pardon some of you, we will punish others among you, as a consequence of their wickedness.

This passage makes it very clear that the Muslim who mocks or jokes about Mohammed has "disbelieved after having believed." The hadiths make it very clear what the penalty is for those who disbelieve after having believed. Consider the following hadiths:

...the prophet said, "if somebody (a Muslim) discards his religion, kill him" (Bukhari 4:260).

Narrated 'Ikrima:

Some Zanadiqa (atheists) were brought to 'Ali and he burnt them. The news of this event, reached Ibn 'Abbas who said, "If I had been in his place, I would not have burnt them, as Allah's Apostle forbade it, saying, 'Do not punish anybody with Allah's punishment (fire).' I would have killed them according to the statement of Allah's Apostle, 'Whoever changed his Islamic religion, then kill him'" (Bukhari 9:57).

Narrated Abu Musa:
A man embraced Islam and then reverted back to Judaism. Mu'adh bin Jabal came and saw the man with Abu Musa. Mu'adh asked, "What is wrong with this (man)?" Abu Musa replied, "He embraced Islam and then reverted back to Judaism." Mu'adh said, "I will not sit down unless you kill him (as it is) the verdict of Allah and His Apostle (Bukhari 9:271).

Narrated 'Ali:
Whenever I tell you a narration from Allah's Apostle, by Allah, I would rather fall down from the sky than ascribe a false statement to him, but if I tell you something between me and you (not a hadith) then it was indeed a trick (i.e., I may say things just to cheat my enemy). No doubt I heard Allah's Apostle saying, "During the last days there will appear some young foolish people who will say the best words but their faith will not go beyond their throats (i.e. they will have no faith) and will go out from (leave) their religion as an arrow goes out of the game. So, where-ever you find them, kill them, for who-ever kills them shall have reward on the Day of Resurrection" (Bukhari 9:64).

In summary, Mohammed supported the murder of the Jews of Qurayza, and the tribe came to an end. Mohammed ordered the murder of men and women who mocked or criticized him. Mohammed declared that Muslims who mocked him were guilty of disbelief and that Muslims who became disbelievers should be killed.

Mohammed cannot support his actions with the Law of Moses or the teachings of Jesus. The only thing that supports the actions of Mohammed are the revelations that Mohammed received. Mohammed said that the angel Gabriel told him to attack the Qurayza, and he said that Allah supported the decision to murder them. Mohammed received the revelation in the Quran that those who mocked him were guilty of disbelief towards Allah and that Muslims who disbelieved should be killed.

17 You Shall Not Lie

Moses taught the Law that God gave him to his followers: "You shall not bear false witness against your neighbor" (Exodus 20:16). "You shall not steal, nor deal falsely, nor lie to one another" (Leviticus 19:11).

It is amazing how seriously the prophets of the Torah took their word. They kept their agreements, oaths, and their covenants even when it was extremely difficult to do so. Joshua kept his covenant of peace with the Gibeonites even when he learned how they had deceived him.

Under the Law of Moses, an oath was considered to be unbreakable. It did not matter how difficult it was to keep an oath, it still needed to be kept. Under the Law of Moses, people feared God. They knew that if they broke their oath, God would be angered.

Jesus taught people not to make special oaths at all. A man should not take special oaths to add weight to his promises. Instead, every word a man speaks should be true. A man should speak good and true words from a good heart.

If we study the life of Mohammed, we soon discover that his covenants and agreements were quickly broken. Mohammed and the Jewish tribes of Medina formed an agreement known as the Constitution of Medina. Mohammed accused the Banu Qaynuqa and the Banu Nadir of breaking the agreement that formed this constitution and he drove them out of the city and took their possessions. Mohammed made a treaty with the Banu Qurayza. After a short time, he accused them of breaking the treaty, and destroyed the tribe. Mohammed entered into a ten-year peace treaty with the Meccans. After two years he accused the Meccans of breaking the treaty and invaded Mecca.

In each case, Muslim scholars have tried to put all the blame upon the tribes who were attacked by Mohammed. In each case, the evidence weighs strongly in the opposite direction. The Muslims broke the oaths and agreements that they made with non-Muslims. The evidence that the Muslims broke their oaths and agreements is not found in the stories of their enemies. The evidence that it was the Muslims who broke their oaths and agreements is found in the writings of the Muslims themselves. The evidence is found in the Sirat, the hadiths, and the Quran itself.

MOHAMMED IS ALLOWED TO BREAK HIS PROMISES

There is a passage in the Quran that states that Mohammed is permitted by Allah to dissolve his oaths. Of course, the one who received this revelation was Mohammed.

Quran 66:1-6 SHAKIR

O Prophet! why do you forbid (yourself) that which Allah has made lawful for you; you seek to please your wives; and Allah is Forgiving, Merciful.

Allah indeed has sanctioned for you the expiation of your oaths and Allah is your Protector, and He is the Knowing the Wise.

And when the prophet secretly communicated a piece of information to one of his wives-- but when she informed (others) of it, and Allah made him to know it, he made known part of it and avoided part; so when he informed her of it, she said: Who informed you of this? He said: The Knowing, the one Aware, informed me.

If you both turn to Allah, then indeed your hearts are already inclined (to this); and if you back up each other against him, then surely Allah it is Who is his Guardian, and Jibreel and -the believers that do good, and the angels after that are the aiders.

Maybe, his Lord, if he divorce you, will give him in your place wives better than you, submissive, faithful, obedient, penitent, adorers, fasters, widows and virgins.

O you who believe! Save yourselves and your families from a fire whose fuel is men and stones; over it are angels stern and strong, they do not disobey Allah in what He commands them, and do as they are commanded.

The first four verses are translated by Yusufali this way:

Quran 66:1-4 YUSUFALI

O Prophet! Why holdest thou to be forbidden that which Allah has made lawful to thee? Thou seekest to please thy consorts. But Allah is Oft-Forgiving, Most Merciful.

Allah has already ordained for you, (O men), the dissolution of your oaths (in some cases): and Allah is your Protector, and He is Full of Knowledge and Wisdom.

When the Prophet disclosed a matter in confidence to one of his consorts, and she then divulged it (to another), and Allah made it known to him, he confirmed part thereof and repudiated a part. Then when he told her thereof, she said, "Who told thee this? "He said, "He told me Who knows and is well-acquainted (with all things)."

If ye two turn in repentance to Him, your hearts are indeed so inclined; But if ye back up each other against him, truly Allah is his Protector, and Gabriel, and (every) righteous one among those who believe,- and furthermore, the angels - will back (him) up.

Why does Allah grant Mohammed the "expiation" or "dissolution" of his oaths? Moses taught his followers that they must keep their oaths. Moses said, "This is the thing which the LORD has commanded, 'If a man makes a vow to the LORD, or swears an oath to bind himself by some agreement, he

145

shall not break his word; he shall do according to all that proceeds out of his mouth"' (Numbers 30:1-2).

Muslim scholars teach that a Muslim can escape his oaths by making "expiation" for them by paying a form of atonement for them. For example, a Muslim who wants to be freed from his oath might feed or clothe ten poor people or free a slave. After doing this, he is freed from his oath.

As is the case with much of the Quran, there is a story that goes together with this passage that helps us to understand it better. The following two hadiths provide evidence that the story is true:

> It was narrated from Anas, that the Messenger of Allah had a female slave with whom he had intercourse, but Aishah and Hafsah would not leave him alone until he said that she was forbidden for him. Then Allah, the Mighty and Sublime, revealed: "O Prophet! Why do you forbid (for yourself) that which Allah has allowed to you" [66:1] until the end of the verse (Sunan An-Nasa'i 3411).

> Narrated 'Abdullah bin 'Abbas:…The Prophet did not go to his wives because of the secret which Hafsa had disclosed to 'Aisha, and he said that he would not go to his wives for one month as he was angry with them when Allah admonished him (for his oath that he would not approach Maria). When twenty-nine days had passed, the Prophet went to Aisha first of all…(Bukhari 3:648)

The Tafsir Jalalayn expounds on the verse this way:

> O Prophet! Why do you prohibit what God has made lawful for you, in terms of your Coptic handmaiden Māriya — when he lay with her in the house of Hafsa, who had been away, but who upon returning [and finding out] became upset by the fact that this had taken place in her own house and on her own bed — by saying, 'She is unlawful for me!', seeking, by making her unlawful [for you], to please your wives? And God is Forgiving, Merciful, having forgiven you this prohibition.

If we read these sources, we begin to understand the story behind the Quranic verses. Mohammed had many wives who were often in conflict with one another. In order to reduce these conflicts, on each day a different wife was given a turn with Mohammed. One day it was Hafsah's "turn" to be with Mohammed but when Mohammed came to her house, she had left the house. Mohammed did not like waiting to satisfy his sexual desires, so he took Mary, the slave girl, into Hafsah's bed and had sex with her. When Hafsah returned, she discovered that Mohammed had slept with the slave girl in her own bed. Hafsah was extremely angry and offended. Not only did she need to share Mohammed with his other wives. Now she even had to share him with the slave girl, Mary. This did not take place somewhere outside of her home. It took place in her own bed.

Mohammed tried to calm Hafsah down. He knew that if his other wives learned that he had slept in Hafsah's bed with the slave girl, all of them would become angry. Hafsah refused to listen. She told Aisha what had happened. Now Mohammed had two angry wives.

Mohammed made an oath to Hafsah and Aisha that he would never again sleep with Mary, the slave girl, if only they would keep quiet about what had happened. He swore that Mary was "forbidden" for him, like a married woman would be.

Even with these promises, Hafsah and Aisha did not keep quiet. As word spread among the wives of Mohammed, the controversy became so heated that many feared that Mohammed would divorce all his wives. Instead of divorcing them, Mohammed left his wives for a month time and moved in with Mary, the slave girl, breaking his oath to Hafsah.

And so the revelation came to Mohammed, that Allah permitted him to break his oaths. In the revelation, Allah rebukes Mohammed and asks him, "O Prophet! why do you forbid (yourself) that which Allah has made lawful for you; you seek to please your wives and Allah is Forgiving, Merciful."

According to this revelation, it was not wrong for Mohammed to sleep with the slave girl in his wife's own bed. The only thing Mohammed did wrong was to promise his wife that he would stop sleeping with the slave girl. Allah rebukes Mohammed for trying to please his wives with an oath instead of simply obeying his lust for the slave girl. He is rebuked for forbidding himself the pleasure of having sex with Mary when it was lawful for him to do so.

The following verses in this passage from the Quran instruct Aisha and Hafsah to turn to Allah and repent and warns them not to support each other in their dispute against Mohammed. If they unite against Mohammed, they will discover that Allah is on Mohammed's side. The Quran warns them that if Mohammed decides to divorce them, Allah will give Mohammed better wives in their place who are more submissive, obedient, and faithful. The next verse warns them about hellfire.

Muslims believe that the Quran is God's eternal word, perfect in heaven, written before the world was created. If this is true, then before the earth was created, God decided to get involved in a fight between Mohammed and his wives. He decided to give Mohammed the right to break his promises to his wives so that he could continue sleeping with his slave girl.

THE TREATY OF HUDAYBIYYAH

Mohammed believed that God allowed him to break his oaths, agreements, and treaties. Mohammed behaved with cruelty and brutality towards those who broke their agreements with him, but he felt that God allowed him to break his oaths with others.

This can be seen in the events surrounding the treaty of Hudaybiyyah. During the time when Mohammed and his followers were exiled from Mecca and living in Medina, Mohammed received a dream in which he saw himself going on a pilgrimage to Mecca to perform Tawaf around the Kaaba. After receiving this vision, Mohammed and his men traveled to Mecca, but the Meccans refused to allow them to enter the city. At this time the Meccans were stronger than Mohammed and his followers.

Instead of fighting the Meccans, Mohammed and his men made a treaty of peace with them known as the treaty of Hudaybiyyah. In this treaty, the two sides agreed not to take up arms against each other for ten years. In this agreement, Mohammed agreed that he would send back to Mecca anyone who tried to leave Mecca to join him, but anyone who left Mohammed and arrived in Mecca could remain in Mecca. It was agreed that Mohammed and his men would not be permitted to enter Mecca that year, but in the following year he could enter Mecca with his men to perform the ceremonies at the Kaaba.

Soon after the treaty was made, a woman named Umm Kulthum Uqba left Mecca to join Mohammed. According to the treaty, she needed to be sent back to Mecca. When her brothers arrived in Medina to demand her return, Mohammed refused to honor the terms of the treaty. He decided that women who wanted to join him from Mecca were free to join him, so long as their dowries were paid back to the ones whom they left.

Mohammed received a revelation supporting his decision to break the treaty.

> O you who believe, when believing women (abandon the enemy and) ask for asylum with you, you shall test them. GOD is fully aware of their belief. Once you establish that they are believers, you shall not return them to the disbelievers. They are not lawful to remain married to them, nor shall the disbelievers be allowed to marry them. Give back the dowries that the disbelievers have paid. You commit no error by marrying them, so long as you pay them their due dowries. Do not keep disbelieving wives (if they wish to join the enemy). You may ask them for the dowry you had paid, and they may ask for what they paid. This is GOD's rule; He rules among you. GOD is Omniscient, Most Wise. (Quran 60:10 Rashad)

This passage declares that if a married woman wants to join Mohammed without her husband, then her marriage is no longer lawful in the sight of Allah. She is free to join Mohammed and marry a Muslim.

The treaty of Hudaybiyyah was binding upon the Meccans, the Muslims, and the tribes who were allied with either side. A man named Abu Basir organized raids against the Meccans during the days that the treaty was in effect (Bukhari 3:891). Abu Basir became a Muslim and killed a Meccan. Mohammed sent him to the coast, where he formed a band of seventy Muslims who survived by raiding the Meccan caravans. They murdered Meccans and stole their property, during the time that the treaty was in effect.

In these ways, Mohammed and his followers broke the treaty of Hudaybiyyah, while the Meccans tried to keep the peace, and did not declare war.

A tribe known as the Banu Bakr joined the side of the Meccans and a tribe known as the Khuza'a joined the Muslims. Before these two tribes joined their partners, revenge killings were taking place between the two tribes. If a member of one tribe was murdered, that tribe would try to murder a member of the tribe who committed the murder. These revenge killings continued after the Banu Bakr joined the Muslims. The Banu Bakr sought revenge against the Khuza'a, and killed several members of that tribe. Today Muslims blame the Meccans for breaking the treaty of Hudaybiyyah, because of these killings committed by Mecca's allies. In fact, the Quran and Bukhari testify that the treaty was actually broken by Mohammed and the Muslims before these killings ever took place.

Mohammed used the time of peace that the treaty provided to strengthen his army. When he felt strong enough, he blamed the Meccans for breaking the treaty and invaded Mecca. This invasion took place less than two years after he had signed the treaty of Hudaybiyyah, in which he had promised to keep peace for 10 years.

When Mohammed broke an oath or a treaty, he always blamed the other party and claimed that God told him to do whatever he did. It was God who wanted Mohammed to break his oath with his wives so that he could continue sleeping with the slave girl. It was God who led Mohammed to break his treaty with the Meccans so that their woman could break their marriages and join him.

Naturally, Mohammed's men learned from Mohammed. Abu Bakr, who became caliph of the Muslims when Mohammed died, said:

> "If I take an oath to do something and later on I find something else better than the first one, then I do what is better and make expiation for my oath" (Bukhari 78:618).

In other words, when it became inconvenient for Abu Bakr to carry out his oath, he simply performed a good deed as "expiation" for his oath. Then he was free to break his word and do what he wanted to do. This was the way of Mohammed, and it is the way of his followers. If you follow Mohammed's example, you will break your word when it is convenient for you to do so.

God is not a follower of Mohammed. He does not break his word. He keeps his promises. He has stated in his word that all liars will be cast into the lake of fire.

But the cowardly, unbelieving, abominable, murderers, sexually immoral, sorcerers, idolaters, and all liars shall have their part in the lake which burns with fire and brimstone, which is the second death" (Revelation 21:8).

18 You Shall Not Covet

Moses taught his followers "You shall not covet." A man was not to covet his neighbor's wife, nor his servants, nor his ox, nor his donkey, nor anything that belonged to his neighbor (Exodus 20:17).

Jesus warned men of covetousness. Jesus spoke to the man who thought his brother was cheating him in the matter of his inheritance. He said to him, "Beware of covetousness. For a man's life 'does not consist in the abundance of his possessions." Jesus knew that the man had focused his heart on the money that his brother had taken. Jesus knew that this man had made an idol of that money in his heart and that he was beginning to covet that money.

The Christian Bible teaches that covetousness is a form of idolatry (Colossians 3:5). When men covet something, they do not bow down to an idol made of stone or wood. When men covet something, they serve an idol that is in their heart. They desire something in their heart that does not belong to them. They lust after that thing. In the eyes of God, they are committing idolatry.

GOLD, GIRLS, AND GLORY

It is said that men crave three things, the 3 g's: gold, girls, and glory. Men desire wealth, they desire women, and they desire glory or the praise of man. The lust for these things is the lust of the flesh. It is covetousness. It is idolatry.

These idols of the heart are never satisfied. The man who covets money will never be satisfied with money. He will always lust after more money. The man who covets women will never be satisfied with a woman. After he fulfills his lust, it will grow in him again. The man who covets the glory and praise of men will never be satisfied. He will always want more.

This is what happened to Mohammed. No matter how many women Mohammed had, he did not stop coveting women who did not belong to him. Mohammed was a wealthy man, but he coveted his neighbors' possessions. He coveted their gold, their livestock, their wives, and their servants. Mohammed received an incredible amount of praise and honor from his followers, but he coveted more. He became enraged and condemned to death those who mocked him or criticized him.

Covetousness is idolatry. The covetous person might claim to be serving God. He might be very religious. He might appear to pray in a perfect manner. But what is in his heart? If the desires of the flesh burn in that person's heart, he has become an idolater. Mohammed broke the idols that were in the Kaaba, but he did not break the idols that lived in people's hearts.

MOHAMMED AND WOMEN

Covetousness is hidden in a person's heart, and it is never possible to fully know what is in the heart. However, people give us clues to what is in their hearts through their words and their deeds. A person's words and deeds reveal to some extent the idols that live in their hearts.

In the case of Mohammed, it seems that Mohammed coveted women. When it comes to things of this world, Mohammed loved horses and perfume, but even more than these, he loved women. Consider the following hadiths:

Al-Fadl lbn Dukayn informed us: Musa Ibn Qays al-Hadrami informed us on the authority of Salamah ibn Kuhayl; he said: The Apostle of Allah, may Allah bless him, did not obtain anything from worldly objects dearer to him than women and perfumes (Kitab al-Tabaqat al-Kabir Volume 1, Parts II.90.5).

`Affan Ibn Muslim informed us: Abu Hilal informed us on the authority of Qatadah, he on the authority of Ma'qil ibn Yasar; he said: Nothing was dearer to the Prophet of Allah, may Allah bless him, than a horse. Then he said: 0 Allah! excuse me, nay! the women (i.e. not dearer than women) (Kitab al-Tabaqat al-Kabir Volume 1, Parts II.90.6).

Hadiths such as the ones above indicate that Mohammed may have coveted women. Mohammed's actions also indicate that he coveted women. We have already described what took place between Mohammed and the wife of his adopted son, Zaid. Mohammed saw Zaynab in a barely dressed state. He desired her, even though she did not belong to him. He claimed that Allah was the one who put this desire in his heart. Zaid realized that Mohammed coveted his wife, and he divorced her so that Mohammed could marry her.

Of course, a covetous man is not easily satisfied. When it came to women, Mohammed was not easily satisfied. He claimed to have the sexual stamina of 40 men. The following hadith shows that even when Mohammed had nine wives, he would try to visit them all in one night.

Narrated Anas bin Malik: The Prophet used to pass by (have sexual relation with) all his wives in one night, and at that time he had nine wives (Bukhari 7:142).

After the battle of Khaybar, one of Mohammed's soldiers named Dihya said to him, "O Allah's prophet! Give me a slave girl from the captives." Mohammed replied, "Go and take any slave girl." Dihya chose for himself Safiyya bint Huyay.

Some of the men knew how beautiful Safiyya was. One of Mohammed's men came to Mohammed and said to him, "O Allah's Apostles! You gave Safiyya bint Huyayy to Dihya and she is the chief mistress of the tribes of Qurayza and An-Nadir and she befits none but you."

When Mohammed heard how beautiful Safiyya was, he coveted her. Even though he had already given her away to Dihya, he decided that he should have her for himself. Mohammed called Diya and told him that he could choose another female captive for himself, but that he was taking Safiyya (Bukhari 1:367).

The Quran teaches that a Muslim man can have up to four wives (Quran 4:3), so long as he is able to treat them justly. Mohammed had nine wives when he died. Muslims explain this contradiction in different ways. Some claim that the extra marriages were necessary for forming alliances with various tribes. Others claim that Allah favored Mohammed above ordinary men, and allowed him to take as many wives as he liked.

Mohammed received another revelation that is written in the Quran that states that he is allowed to take any woman he chooses, so long as she is not "forbidden" to him.

> O Prophet (Muhammad)! Verily, We have made lawful to you: your wives to whom you have paid their dowers; and those whom your right hand possesses out of the prisoners of war whom Allah has assigned to you; and daughters of your paternal uncles and aunts and daughters of your maternal uncles and aunts who migrated (from Makkah) with you; and any believing woman who dedicates her soul to the Prophet if the Prophet wishes to wed her. This is only for you and not for the Believers (at large). We know what We have appointed for them as to their wives and the captives whom their right hands possess in order that there should be no difficulty for you. And Allah is Most Forgiving, Most Merciful.
>
> **You may put off whom you please of them, and you may take to you whom you please, and whom you desire of those whom you had separated provisionally; no blame attaches to you**; this is most proper, so that their eyes may be cool and they may not grieve, and that they should be pleased, all of them with what you give them, and Allah knows what is in your hearts; and Allah is Knowing, Forbearing (Quran 33:50-51).

According to these verses, Mohammed may marry any believing woman who dedicates her soul to him. He can take to himself the one he wishes, and no blame will be attached to him. These verses make it very clear that this opportunity is only allowed for Mohammed and not for the believers.

Verse 52 seems to contradict verses 50 and 51:

> (33:52) Beyond the categories described to you, you are enjoined from marrying any other women, nor can you substitute a new wife (from the prohibited categories), no matter how much you admire their beauty. You must be content with those already made lawful to you. **GOD** is watchful over all things.

Some scholars believe that verse 50 abrogates, or cancels out verse 52. In other words, the revelation that Mohammed can take any woman who dedicates her soul to him overrules the verse that tells him to be satisfied with the wives he has.

Aisha didn't like the fact that woman would come to Mohammed and give themselves to him. She found it strange that Allah so quickly agreed to allow Mohammed to have these women, even though the Quran said that it was not ok. She made a comment about this part of the Quran which is found in the following hadith:

> Aisha (Allah be pleased with her) reported: "I felt jealous of the women who offered themselves to Allah's Messenger (may peace be upon him) and said: Then when Allah, the Exalted and Glorious, revealed this: 'You may defer any one of them you wish, and take to yourself any you wish; and if you desire any you have set aside (no sin is chargeable to you)' (xxxiii. 51), I ('Aisha.) said: It seems to me that your Lord hastens to satisfy your desire" (Muslim 3453).

Aisha understood that Mohammed desired these women who came to him. She understood that he coveted them. She found it strange that Allah so quickly gave Mohammed a revelation that satisfied his sexual desires.

THE HOURIS OF HEAVEN

The Christian Bible teaches that the rewards of heaven are beyond a man's comprehension. It is written, "Eye has not seen, nor ear heard, nor have entered into the heart of man the things which God has prepared for those who love him" (I Corinthians 2:9).

Jesus said, "In My Father's house are many mansions; if it were not so, I would have told you. I go to prepare a place for you. And if I go and prepare a place for you, I will come again and receive you to myself; that where I am, there you may be also" (John 14:2-3).

Jesus also taught that there is no marriage in heaven. He rebuked men who thought they would have wives in heaven saying, "Are you not therefore mistaken, because you do not know the Scriptures nor the power of God? For when (men) rise from the dead, they neither marry nor are given in marriage, but are like angels in heaven" (Mark 12:25).

Mohammed desired women so much, that he could not imagine heaven without sexual intercourse. As usual, he received revelations that matched his desires. He received the revelation that in heaven a man will receive 72 beautiful virgins, created especially for him as companions. They will be pure. They will be holy. They will have beautiful breasts. And of course, a man can have sex with them.

> We created the Houris and made them virgins, loving companions for those of the right hand... That Which is Coming,... (Quran 56:36, Dawud).

> As for the righteous, they shall surely triumph. Theirs shall be gardens and vineyards, and high-bosomed virgins for companions: a truly overflowing cup (Quran 78:31-33, Dawud).

> "Thus (shall it be), and We will wed them with Houris, pure, beautiful ones" (Quran 44:54, Shakir).

Mohammed also received the revelation that a man's sexual ability would be greatly increased in heaven. He would have the sexual desire of a hundred men, and he would have the strength of a hundred men to engage in sexual intercourse. For a man who coveted women as much as Mohammed did, this would be heaven indeed! In Mohammed's mind, heaven was a place where all his lust would be satisfied.

> A man will have intercourse in Paradise with his wives from among al-hoor al-'iyn and his wives from among the people of this world, if they enter Paradise with him. **A man will be given the strength of a**

hundred men to eat, drink, feel desire and have sexual intercourse. It was narrated from Anas that the Prophet said: "The believer in Paradise will be given such and such strength for sexual intercourse." He was asked, "O Messenger of Allah, will he really be able to do that?" He said, **"He will be given the strength of one hundred (men)"** (Sunan al-Tirmidhi 2459).

MOHAMMED AND HIS NEIGHBORS' POSSESSIONS

Mohammed coveted his neighbors' possessions. The Jews of Medina were a prosperous people. They excelled in agriculture and other enterprises. Compared to the Muslims who emigrated with Mohammed to Medina, the Jews were wealthy. This wealth drew the attention of Mohammed and his followers. As his followers increased in numbers and power, Mohammed looked for excuses that would allow him to drive the Jews out of Medina and take their possessions.

Mohammed drove out the Banu Qaynuqa because a mob from that tribe stoned a Muslim man who had murdered a Jew. He drove out the Banu Nadir because they delayed in paying blood money for two murders committed by one of Mohammed's own soldiers in spite of the fact that they were not even involved in the murder. He completely destroyed the Banu Qurayza because they seemed to remain neutral in the battle against the Meccan Arabs during the Battle of the Trench.

We have already told the story of Kenana, the wealthy Jewish man in Khaybar. Kenana originally came from Medina, where Mohammed and his army were based. He was the treasurer from the tribe of the Banu Nadir. When Mohammed drove the Banu Nadir out of Medina, he allowed them to leave with the possessions that they and their camels could carry.

Did Mohammed covet the possessions of the Jews of the Banu Nadir? It seems that he did. When the Jews left Medina, they left in a great procession, with all their wealth loaded on the camels. The women were dressed in their finest garments and music was played as the tribe carried their wealth out of the city of Medina to the city of Khaybar.

Mohammed remembered the display of wealth that the Jews of the Banu Nadir made as they left Medina. He coveted this wealth. When the time was right, he sent his army to invade Khaybar. After the battle he searched for Kenana the treasurer, who surely knew where the wealth of the Banu Nadir was hidden.

Mohammed instructed his men to torture Kenana to find out where the treasure of the Jews was hidden. If you torture a man to find out where his possessions are, is it not true that you covet those possessions? Mohammed coveted the treasure of Kenana and the Banu Nadir. He coveted their gold and their land. He coveted Kenana's wife. After Kenana was tortured with fire and beheaded, Mohammed took for himself Kenana's wife, Safiyya, and divided his land and possessions among his men.

At Khaybar, Mohammed left the Jews of the Banu Nadir with nothing. This time the Muslims took the gold of the Jews as well as their lands. Mohammed and his men took the Jewish women that they desired as sex slaves. Some of the Jews worked, remaining in Khaybar for a few years, giving the Muslims half of their crops, but after a few years they too were driven away.

Moses commanded his followers: "You shall not covet your neighbor's house; you shall not covet your neighbor's wife, nor his male servant, nor his female servant, nor his ox, nor his donkey, nor anything that is your neighbor's."

Mohammed coveted his neighbors' houses. He coveted his neighbors' wives. He coveted their possessions and their livestock. When he had the opportunity, he took his neighbors' houses for himself. He oversaw the slaughter of his neighbors. He took the prettiest of their wives for himself, and sold the rest into slavery. He took their oxen, their donkeys, and their possessions for himself and his men.

Mohammed was never satisfied. He never felt that he had enough women. He never thought he had enough land. He never thought he had conquered enough. When he conquered one tribe, he immediately set his sights upon the next tribe. He immediately began lusting after the possessions of the next tribe.

This covetousness caused Mohammed to commit abominations. He tortured and murdered. He took women for himself after killing their husbands. After driving men and women from their homes, he still was not satisfied with what he had taken from them. He followed them to their next destination and robbed them again. He was not satisfied until he had taken everything his neighbors owned, even their family members.

This is idolatry. This idolatry is at the heart of Islam. Those who follow the example of the prophet Mohammed will never be satisfied. They will always want more. They will never live at peace with their neighbors. They will always covet their neighbors' possessions. They will always covet the blessings that their neighbors have received from God. They will not be satisfied until they have taken everything that their neighbors own. They will not be satisfied until they have murdered their neighbors or driven them far way.

This is why conflict, war, and poverty afflict so many Islamic nations. The Bible says that as we sow, we shall reap. Those who sow to the flesh will reap destruction. Those who sow bloodshed reap bloodshed. Those who live by the sword, will die by the sword.

Galatians 6:7-8 says:
(7) Do not be deceived, God is not mocked; for whatever a man sows, that he will also reap.
(8) For he who sows to his flesh will of the flesh reap corruption, but he who sows to the Spirit will of the Spirit reap everlasting life.

MOHAMMED COVETS PRAISE.

There is a kind of coveting that is even worse than the coveting of women or possessions. The worst kind of coveting is found in the heart of Satan, who began to covet the place of God and the praises that God received. The words of Satan are recorded in the Christian Bible in the book of Isaiah:

> **How you are fallen from heaven, O Lucifer, son of the morning! How you are cut down to the ground, You who weakened the nations! For you have said in your heart: "I will ascend into heaven, I will exalt my throne above the stars of God; I will also sit on the mount of the congregation On the farthest sides of the north" (Isaiah 14:12-13).**

Jesus taught his followers, "How can you believe, who receive honor from one another, and do not seek the honor that comes from the only God" (John 5:44)?

When a person starts to crave praise, he enters very dangerous territory. Jesus said that the person who receives the honor that comes from other people, without seeking the honor that comes from God, is not a believer.

Did Mohammed covet the praise of man? Mohammed received the revelation in the Quran that if someone criticized him, that man was guilty of disbelief towards Allah. The Muslim who disbelieves Allah is an apostate who must be put to death.

Mohammed ordered the killing of men and women who mocked him with poems. It is obvious that Mohammed believed he should never be mocked or criticized in any way and that anyone who mocked or criticized him should be dealt with in the most severe manner imaginable.

At the same time, Mohammed's followers praised him constantly. When they greeted him, they said, "May my father and my mother be sacrificed for your sake...." They fought over his spit and the water that he used to wash himself with.

Mohammed was not a man who humbled himself, confessed his faults, and repented of them. Mohammed was a man who was praised constantly, a man who reacted with murderous rage when someone mocked or criticized him. Mohammed believed that he spoke for God and that the man who opposed him opposed God.

Covetousness is hidden in a man's heart. Although we can never know for sure what was in Mohammed's heart, his words, actions and revelations reveal a man who craved and coveted the praise of man. Mohammed's words and actions reveal a man who craved and coveted the possessions and wives of his neighbors.

19 Remember the Sabbath Day

Moses taught us that on the Sabbath no man should work, and that if he broke this command, he should be put to death. Jesus taught us about God's higher purpose for the Sabbath. Jesus taught that the Sabbath is God's gift to mankind. Jesus taught us that there are some works that only God can do. He taught us that the Sabbath is a day for people to rest from their works so that they can focus on the works of God and be thankful. God is able to do the things that are impossible for humans. God is able to heal the sick and raise the dead. God is able to save a person from his sins.

Mohammed taught his followers a different revelation. The "Sabbath" of Islam is on Friday instead of Saturday. The Islamic Sabbath is a day of assembly, not a day of rest. It is the day of the week when Muslims are expected to pray at the mosque. The Quran states that Allah never became tired or needed a day of rest; therefore, there is no day that Allah has made holy as a day of rest.

When Mohammed and the Muslims took refuge in Medina, it was a town that had long been dominated by the Jews. The Sabbath of the Jews is on Saturday. Friday was market day for the Jews of Medina. The Jews completed their business dealings and bought the provisions that they needed for the Sabbath on Friday before the Sabbath began. Arabs who lived and traded in Medina also began to use Friday as their market day.

Mohammed needed a day of the week when the Muslims could meet together and worship God together. Friday was market day in Medina. Friday was the day when Muslims came to town to buy and sell their goods. It made sense for Mohammed to meet with his followers on the day when most of them were in town doing business, instead of on another day when they might be tending their farms and flocks in rural areas.

And so at noon on Friday, Muslims were called together for an obligatory weekly meeting. This meeting included a two-part sermon and prayers. It was held at noon because Friday was a market day. In the morning, people were busy in the marketplace. Traveling at night was not very safe, so people needed to leave early in the day to return to their homes. Therefore, in spite of the heat, noon on Friday was the time when people could most easily be assembled.

The Muslim "Sabbath" is not a day of rest but a day of assembly. Muslims are not forbidden to work on Friday. They are expected to leave their marketplace activities for a few hours to attend the assembly. This can be seen in the following verses:

> O ye who believe! When the call is heard for the prayer of the day of congregation, haste unto remembrance of Allah and leave your trading. That is better for you if ye did but know.

> And when the prayer is ended, then disperse in the land and seek of Allah's bounty, and remember Allah much, that ye may be successful (Quran 62:9-10).

In other words, it is expected that people will be working in the marketplace on the day of assembly. They are supposed to leave their work and attend the assembly, and then they can disburse and continue seeking "Allah's bounty" as they continue their normal work.

The Torah states: "And on the seventh day God ended His work which He had done, and He rested on the seventh day from all His work which He had done. Then God blessed the seventh day and sanctified it because in it He rested from all His work which God had created and made (Genesis 2:2-3).

Mohammed prophesied something very different in the Quran. It is written in the name of Allah, "We created the heavens and the earth and all between them in Six Days, nor did any sense of weariness touch Us" (Quran 50:38). In other words, the Quran denies that the Creator ever needed a day of rest.

No day was set apart as a holy day of rest because the Creator never needed such a day.

Did Mohammed keep the commandment of God that is written in the law of Moses? Did he keep the Sabbath? He did not. The meaning of the Sabbath was completely changed. It was no longer a day of rest. Instead, it became a day of assembly, a day when Muslims gathered together for a few hours to pray and listen to a sermon. Even the day was changed. It was changed from Saturday, the day of rest for the Jews, to Friday, market day for Jews and Muslims.

Mohammed justified these changes with a revelation. He received the revelation that Allah had given Friday to the Jews as their Sabbath day, but they argued with Allah and took Saturday instead. And so Allah gave Friday to the Muslims. The fact that Friday comes before Saturday and Sunday is a sign, according to the revelation, that Christians and Jews are behind the Muslims, who will be at the front on the Day of Resurrection.

> Narrated Abu Huraira:
> I heard Allah's Apostle (p.b.u.h) saying, "We (Muslims) are the last (to come) but (will be) the foremost on the Day of Resurrection though the former nations were given the Holy Scriptures before us. And this was their day (Friday) the celebration of which was made compulsory for them but they differed about it. So Allah gave us the guidance for it (Friday) and all the other people are behind us in this respect: the Jews' (holy day is) tomorrow (i.e. Saturday) and the Christians' (is) the day after tomorrow (i.e. Sunday)" (Bukhari 2:1, and 2:21).

Although Mohammed did not keep the Sabbath, it did not keep him from prophesying terrible things about the Jews who broke the Sabbath. Those who received the scriptures (Jews and Christians) are told in the Quran to believe what they have received from God. They are told that Sabbath breakers are cursed.

> O ye unto whom the Scripture hath been given! Believe in what we have revealed confirming that which ye possess, before we destroy countenances so as to confound them, or curse them as we cursed the Sabbath-breakers (of old time), the Commandment of Allah is always executed (Quran 4:47, Pickthal).

The Quran speaks even worse things about those who break the Sabbath:

And ye know of those of you who broke the Sabbath, how We said unto them: Be ye apes, despised and hated! And We made it an example to their own and to succeeding generations, and an admonition to the Allah-fearing (Quran 2:65-66 Pickthal).

It is written in the Quran that Jews are hated and despised apes because they have broken the Sabbath. It is written that Allah hates and despises the Jews because they have broken the Sabbath.

If this is true, how do you think God would see someone who completely changed the meaning of the Sabbath? What would God think about a man who decided to change the day of the Sabbath, moving it from a day that had been set apart for thousands of years as a holy day, and changing it to a market day? If the Jews were cursed because they did not keep the Sabbath properly, what would be done to a man who changed the day of the Sabbath, changed the meaning of the Sabbath, and taught everyone that they must follow his example?

Judgment is without mercy to the one who shows no mercy. Can a man who does not keep the Sabbath judge the Jews because they did not keep the Sabbath properly? The Jews might have broken the Law of Moses. But if you are going to judge the Jews harshly in this way, shouldn't you keep the Sabbath yourself? As Jesus said, "Judge not, that you be not judged. For with what judgment you judge, you will be judged; and with the measure you use, it will be measured back to you" (Matthew 7:1-2).

Everyone has broken the laws of God. Everyone needs grace. According to the Christian Bible, there are certain conditions that must be met for one to receive grace. If a man hopes to be forgiven for his sins, it is necessary that he remember the three things described below.

THE THREE PRINCIPLES OF FORGIVENESS

The first principal of forgiveness is found in these words of Jesus: "For if you forgive men their trespasses, your heavenly Father will also forgive you. But if you do not forgive men their trespasses, neither will your Father forgive your trespasses (Matthew 6:14-15).

The man who hopes to be forgiven by God for his sins must also forgive those who sin against him. If you do not forgive, you will not be forgiven. Judgment is without mercy to the one who shows not mercy.

The second principal of forgiveness is found in the scripture of the Christian Bible that says, "God resists the proud, but gives grace to the humble" (1 Peter 5:5). If you want to receive grace from God, you must humble yourself. If you are a proud man, you will not receive grace and forgiveness from God.

Jesus said, "Everyone who exalts himself will be humbled, and he who humbles himself will be exalted" (Luke 18:14).

Thirdly, if you wish to escape the terrible judgments of God, you must stop judging and condemning others. The way that you judge others will determine the way that you are judged. If you judge harshly, you will also be judged harshly. If you judge without mercy, you will also be judged without mercy. If you desire to receive mercy from God, you must also give mercy to others. Jesus said, "Judge not, that you be not judged. For with what judgment you judge, you will be judged; and with the measure you use, it will be measured back to you" (Matthew 7:1-2).

"For judgment is without mercy to the one who has shown no mercy. Mercy triumphs over judgment" (James 2:13).

Mohammed taught his followers that they were much better than the Jews and Christians, whom he despised as lawbreakers. He called the Jews apes, and declared that they were cursed by God. He declared that his followers were the best of all men, the most righteous in history. Does this sound like pride to you?

Mohammed sought the forgiveness of God for his sins, but he did not forgive those who sinned against him. Mohammed did not forgive his enemies or his neighbors. He cursed his enemies by name at the beginning of each time of prayer. When Mohammed's neighbors surrendered to him, he murdered them. If someone criticized Mohammed with a poem, Mohammed condemned that person to death.

Mohammed believed that he could judge everyone who did not obey him and follow him. He judged and condemned the Jews and killed many of them. He judged and condemned every man who refused to believe in him and follow him.   He judged those who mocked him and condemned them to death.

Mohammed broke the Law of Moses many times, yet he condemned to death the Jewish couple who committed adultery. Mohammed broke the Sabbath and changed its meaning, yet he condemned the Jews who broke the Sabbath.

What do you think will happen to Mohammed on the Day of Judgment?

20 Honor your Father and Mother

The teachings of the Quran and the hadiths regarding honoring one's parents are nearly identical to the teachings of the Torah and the teachings of Jesus. All of these scriptures agree that it is very important to honor one's parents. Here are a few verses from the Quran that speak about honoring one's parents.

> ... You shall regard GOD, by whom you swear, and regard the parents. GOD is watching over you (Quran 4:1, Rashad).

> Say, "Come, let me tell you what your Lord has really prohibited for you: You shall not set up idols besides Him. You shall honor your parents. You shall not kill your children from fear of poverty - we provide for you and for them. You shall not commit gross sins, obvious or hidden. You shall not kill - GOD has made life sacred - except in the course of justice. These are His commandments to you, that you may understand" (Quran 6:151, Rashad).

> Your Lord has decreed that you shall not worship except Him, and your parents shall be honored. As long as one or both of them live, you shall never say to them, "Uff" (the slightest gesture of annoyance), nor shall you shout at them; you shall treat them amicably. And lower for them the wings of humility, and kindness, and say, "My Lord, have mercy on them, for they have raised me from infancy" (Quran 17:23-24, Rashad).

We enjoined the human being to honor his parents. But if they try to force you to set up idols beside Me, do not obey them. To Me is your ultimate return, then I will inform you of everything you had done (Quran 29:8, Rashad).

"Honor your father and your mother, that your days may be long upon the land which the LORD your God is giving you" (Exodus 20:12).

It seems that on this point, Moses, Jesus and Mohammed are in complete agreement. However, there is one problem that comes up when you read the different scriptures. Moses taught, "And he who curses his father or his mother shall surely be put to death." Jesus denounced religious men who pretended to honor God as they dishonored their parents. These religious men used to say to their parents, "The honor I would have given to you, I am giving to God instead" (Matt. 14:4,5). After making this statement, these men would give nothing to their parents, but would give everything to God.

If you read the hadiths, you will realize that something very similar took place every day during the time of Mohammed. When people greeted Mohammed, they usually greeted him with the words, "May my father and mother be sacrificed for you." In other words, they honored Mohammed far above their parents, to the degree that they wished their parents would be killed for Mohammed's sake. Instead of rebuking these people for dishonoring their parents in this way, Mohammed received these greetings every day.

Is this not a kind of curse? If a man truly honors his parents, will he propose that they be killed for the sake of a prophet? During the days of Moses, such a greeting would have been unthinkable.

A greeting such as the one above sounds very religious because it exalts the prophet far above one's parents. In fact, the one who makes it is breaking the fifth commandment. He is dishonoring his parents. The fact that these greetings took place so many times is evidence that Mohammed encouraged this kind of greeting. Therefore, he is also not without guilt in this matter.

When we look at Mohammed's life, it is not enough to look at his words. It is necessary to look at his actions. If you say you are against rape and murder, and yet you commit rape and murder, you are still a rapist and a murderer. If you say you are against lying, but you tell lies, you are still a liar. And if you teach people to honor their parents, while encouraging everyone to curse their parents when they greet you, are you really innocent?

21 You Shall Not Make for Yourself an Idol

The Law of Moses forbids covetousness, which involves the idols of the heart. Jesus said, "No one can serve two masters; for either he will hate the one and love the other, or else he will be loyal to the one and despise the other. You cannot serve God and money" (Matthew 6:24).

The Law of Moses also forbids bowing down to idols made of wood and stone. It states, "You shall not make for yourself a carved image—any likeness of anything that is in heaven above, or that is in the earth beneath, or that is in the water under the earth; you shall not bow down to them nor serve them. For I, the Lord your God, am a jealous God..." (Exodus 20:4-5).

God hates idolatry. Every idol represents evil spirits that are in rebellion against God. Every culture and every tribe has worshiped these spirits in times past. These spirits demand that people perform rituals that please them.

These spirits demand sacrifices; because when blood is shed, a blood covenant is formed between the worshiper and the evil spirit that is being worshipped. The evil spirit becomes the "god" of the worshiper. The worshiper gives himself to his god in covenant.

This is why God speaks of His jealousy when He condemns idolatry. The man who worships an idol enters into a covenant with an evil spirit. That spirit becomes his god, and the anger of the true God is stirred up.

IDOL WORSHIPING ARABS

Before the time of Islam, the Arabs were idol worshipers. For many generations, the Arabs bowed down to idols and worshiped them. These idols were a snare and a bondage to the Arab people.

In particular, the Arabs worshiped stones during those days. When they found a stone they thought was better than one that they already had, they would throw out the old one and replace it with the new one (Bukhari 6:661). They used these stones as idols.

Before worshiping their stones and their idols, the Arabs would enter a "sacred" state known as Ihram. To enter this state, they would perform ritual washings to cleanse themselves before their acts of worship. Sometimes they would wear special garments as a part of the worship. For example, the Arabs used to enter "Ihram" before they worshipped the idol Manat.

> Narrated 'Urwa: I asked 'Aisha : ...But in fact, this divine inspiration was revealed concerning the Ansar who used to assume "Ihram" for worshipping an idol called "Manat" which they used to worship at a place called Al-Mushallal before they embraced Islam, and whoever assumed Ihram (for the idol), would consider it not right to perform Tawaf between Safa and Marwah (Bukhari 2:703).

The Arabs of Mecca had a holy shrine where they kept their idols known as the Kaaba. The Kaaba was home to 360 idols. Built into the eastern corner of the Kaaba was a black stone that was highly revered by the Arabs. Mohammed himself set the black stone in the wall of the Kaaba before the time when he began to receive his revelations. Mohammed's tribe, the Quraysh, was the priestly tribe that directed the rituals of the Kaaba during the time of Mohammed (570–630 AD).

The Arabs performed animal sacrifices as they worshiped their stones, idols, and evil spirits at the Kaaba. They smeared the blood of sacrificed animals on the stones. As they did so, they formed a blood covenant with the evil spirits that they were worshiping. In the spirit realm, they made a connection between themselves and these spirits. In the spirit realm they declared that they belonged to these evil spirits as they smeared the blood upon the stones.

Before the days of Islam, the Arabs performed Tawaf around the Kaaba. As they circled the Kaaba, they used to kiss the black stone as they passed it. As they marched around the Kaaba they called out the names of their false gods, just as Muslims call out Allah's name today.

Before the days of Islam, the Arabs also performed Tawaf around the two hills known as Safa and Marwa. They walked in circles around these two hills as a part of their pagan ceremonies. In those days, Arabs would often perform Tawaf while naked.

The main false god that was worshiped at the Kaaba was Hubal, the moon god. The crescent moon was the symbol for Hubal. The Arabs also worshiped the goddesses al-Lat, al-Uzza and Manat at the Kaaba. These three goddesses are mentioned in the Quran.

These false gods spoke through the Arab diviners. Sometimes these false gods demanded blood sacrifices, even human sacrifices. On one occasion these false gods even demanded the sacrifice of Abdullah, Mohammed's father, when he was a young boy. Abdullah's father took him to the Kaaba to offer him as a sacrifice. Before he was killed, they decided to consult another diviner, a woman. This woman consulted the evil spirits and they agreed to accept one hundred camels instead of the life of Abdullah. So the camels were sacrificed in Abdullah's place (Ibn Hasham).

The pre-Islamic condition of ignorance was a terrible time indeed. The Arab people were deeply bound by evil spirits and idolatry. They were deeply involved in pagan rituals. Mohammed brought monotheism and Islam to the Arabs, and it seemed that paganism would disappear forever.

MOHAMMED CONQUERS MECCA

On December 11, 629, Mohammed entered Mecca with his army of 10,000 Muslim warriors. Very little fighting took place before the pagan Arabs of Mecca surrendered to Mohammed's army. Mohammed's main rival, Abu

Sufyan, became a Muslim. He admitted that the Meccan gods were powerless against Mohammed's army, and that there was "no god but Allah."

Then Mohammed and his companions visited the Kaaba. Around the Kaaba 360 idols were positioned. Mohammed carried a stick. He began to stab the idols with his stick as he declared, "Truth (Islam) has come and falsehood (disbelief) has vanished." The idols were broken and smashed (Bukhari 3:658).

The people of Mecca assembled, and Mohammed spoke to them:

"There is no God but Allah. He has no associate. He has made good His promise that He held to his bondman and helped him and defeated all the confederates. Bear in mind that every claim of privilege, whether that of blood or property is abolished except that of the custody of the Kaaba and of supplying water to the pilgrims…."

In this way Islam was established in Mecca, and the Kaaba was cleansed of idols. However, although Mohammed changed the religious doctrines of the Arabs, many of the old ceremonies continued in nearly the same form. The Kaaba is still the center of Islamic worship, just as it was during the days of idol worship. Muslims bow down in the direction of the Kaaba five times a day. Muslims still go on pilgrimage to the Kaaba. This pilgrimage is a central part of Islam. It is one of the five pillars of Islam.

When an Arab Muslim goes on Hajj today, he performs Tawaf around the Kaaba, just like his idol-worshiping ancestors did. He still kisses the black stone, just like his idol-worshiping ancestors did. He still performs Tawaf around the hills of Safa and Marwa, just as his idol-worshiping ancestors did. Just as the idol-worshiping Arabs used to enter a state of Ihram before worshiping Manat, Muslims still enter a state of Ihram before going on pilgrimage to the Kaaba.

Animal sacrifices are still performed today as part of the ceremonies of Hajj. On the third day of Hajj, the pilgrim is required to make an animal sacrifice if he is able to afford it. The pilgrim sacrifices a cow, a sheep, or a camel. Today, most pilgrims buy sacrifice vouchers when they arrive in Mecca, which allows an animal to be sacrificed in their name.

Why did these pagan practices continue? These are the ceremonies of idol worship. These ceremonies took place for many generations as Arabs worshiped stones, idols, and false gods. Why should God be worshiped in this way today?

REVELATIONS

The reason for the continuance of these Kaaba ceremonies is very simple. Mohammed received revelations that supported the continued use of these ceremonies. For example, during pre-Islamic times, the Muslims performed Tawaf around Safa and Marwa. When Islam came, some Muslims thought that these pagan ceremonies should cease.

But then Mohammed received the revelation that these two mountains were actually symbols of Allah, and that it was therefore not a sin to perform Tawaf between them:

> Narrated 'Asim: I asked Anas bin Malik: "Did you use to dislike to perform Tawaf between Safa and Marwa?" He said, "Yes, as it was of the ceremonies of the days of the Pre-lslamic period of ignorance, till Allah revealed: 'Verily! (The two mountains) As-Safa and Al-Marwa are among the symbols of Allah. It is therefore no sin for him who performs the pilgrimage to the Ka'ba, or performs 'Umra, to perform Tawaf between them' " (Quran 2:158, Bukhari 2:710).

Mohammed told his followers a story to support the Tawaf of Safa and Marwa. He declared that when Hagar and Ishmael were abandoned in the desert by Abraham, Hagar ran seven times between these two mountains until she found the Zamzam well (Bukhari 4:583). Therefore, Muslims should perform Tawaf between these two mountains to remember what she did.

Why were animal sacrifices still a part of the worship ceremonies that took place at the Kaaba? God spoke through his prophets long ago that he no longer desires the blood of sheep and cows (Isaiah 1:11, Psalms 50:13). God desires a better sacrifice, a perfect sacrifice that can fully pay the price of sin. So why should the blood of animals continue to be shed during worship?

Muslims are taught that these animal sacrifices are necessary to remind them of the story of Abraham and Ishmael. Mohammed received the revelation that Ishmael was the chosen son of Abraham, and that God told Abraham to offer Ishmael as a sacrifice to test him (Quran 37:99-106). When God saw that Abraham was willing to sacrifice his son, he gave Abraham another sacrifice to use in place of his son.

Another question arose. Why should Muslims kiss the black stone? Pagan Arabs worshiped stones, and they kissed and revered the black stone that was set in the corner of the Kaaba. Why should the true God be worshiped in the same way?

Quite simply, Mohammed kissed the black stone, and Muslims today follow his example.

> It was narrated that Ibn 'Abbaas said: The Messenger of Allah (peace and blessings of Allah be upon him) performed Tawaaf on his camel, and every time he came to the corner [where the Stone is] he would point to it and say "Allaahu akbar" (Bukhari 2:681).

Mohammed declared that the black stone came down to earth from Paradise. It landed at the exact spot where the Kaaba was to be built (al-Tirmidhi 877, al-Nasaa'i, 2935). Mohammed also stated concerning the stone, "By Allah, Allah will bring it forth on the Day of Resurrection, and it will have two eyes with which it will see and a tongue with which it will speak, and it will testify in favor of those who touched it in sincerity" (al-Tirmidhi 961, Ibn Maajah 2944).

Umar, the second caliph, evidently also questioned whether it was really appropriate to kiss the stone. He said to the stone: "I know that you are a stone that neither helps nor hurts, and if the messenger of god had not kissed you, I would not kiss you" (Bukhari 2:667).

Why has this house of idols received such a central position in Islam? Mohammed received revelations about this house that are written in the Quran. Mohammed claimed that the Kaaba was a sacred house ordained by Allah to bring blessing and guidance for mankind (Quran 5:97). He told his followers that the Kaaba was actually built by Abraham and Ishmael. Ishmael brought the rocks for the building, and Abraham did the construction itself (B4:583). As they raised the foundations, Abraham prayed, "Our Lord! Accept from us (this duty). Lo! Thou, only Thou, art the Hearer, the Knower (Quran 2:127 Pickthal).

ABRAHAM COULD NOT HAVE BUILT KAABA

Mohammed's own testimony shows that it isn't possible that Abraham built the Kaaba. Mohammed claimed that the Kaaba was actually the first house of worship built for mankind (Quran 3:96). He claimed the second mosque was Solomon's temple in Jerusalem. He claimed that the period between the construction of the two mosques was forty years.

> Narrated Abu Dhaar: I said, "O Allah's Apostle! Which mosque was built first?" He replied, "Al-Masjid-ul-Haram." I asked, "Which (was built) next?" He replied, "Al-Masjid-ul-Aqs-a (i.e. Jerusalem)." I asked, "What was the period in between them? He replied, forty years (Bukhari 4:636).

Biblical scholars believe that Solomon's temple was built in Jerusalem at approximately 955 BC. Therefore, according to Mohammed, the Kaaba was built forty years earlier, or approximately 995 BC. However, Abraham lived more than a thousand years before this time, at approximately 2000 BC. So how could the Kaaba have been built by Abraham 40 years before the building of Solomon's temple? Abraham had already been dead for more than a thousand years when Solomon's temple was built.

The only evidence that the Kaaba was built by Abraham and Ishmael is Mohammed's word. There is no archaeological or historical evidence that the Kaaba even existed more than a few hundred years before Mohammed's lifetime. The Old Testament of the Bible describes Abraham's life in much detail, but it speaks nothing about Abraham coming to Mecca to build a temple. Abraham never built a temple. He herded his sheep in the land of Canaan (modern Israel), not in Arabia. The altars that Abraham and his sons built were also in Canaan, not in Arabia.

MOHAMMED CREATES NEW STORIES

To a large degree, Mohammed kept the pagan Arab rituals, but he created new stories to go with those rituals. In pre-Islamic times, Arabs worshiped at the Kaaba, kissed the black stone, and performed Tawaf. The evil spirits that were associated with their idols instructed them how to perform these rituals. The evil spirits instructed them how to enter a state of Ihram, how to wash themselves and to perform their ceremonies in an acceptable manner. The evil spirits demanded blood sacrifices. These rituals were performed in honor of Hubal, al-Lat, al-Uzza, Manat and other false gods.

Mohammed knew that if he wanted Arab support for his new religion, it was important that he allow the Arabs to continue their traditional ceremonies. On one occasion Mohammed stated that the reason he kept the Kaaba intact was that the Arabs were still close too close to their pre-Islamic condition. If he made too many changes to their traditional rituals, he feared that they might not accept his new religion of Islam. This can be seen in the following hadith:

> Narrated Aswad: Ibn Az-Zubair said to me, "Aisha used to tell you secretly a number of things. What did she tell you about the Ka'ba?" I replied, "She told me that once the Prophet said, 'O 'Aisha! Had not your people been still close to the pre-Islamic period of ignorance (infidelity)! I would have dismantled the Ka'ba and would have made two doors in it; one for entrance and the other for exit." Later on Ibn Az-Zubair did the same (Bukhari 1:128).

Mohammed received revelations that permitted the Arabs to continue these ceremonies. He helped to change the stories that were associated with these rituals. He made it clear that God wanted these rituals that were previously used to worship idols to continue.

Mohammed spoke in the name of Allah, saying that it was Allah's will for the Kaaba, the house of idols to be at the very center of Islamic worship. Mohammed spoke in the name of Allah and said that this house of idols was a holy house. Mohammed spoke in the name of Allah and said that the pagan ceremonies such as the Tawaf around As-Safa and Al-Marwah were actually ceremonies that received Allah's support. Animal sacrifices were necessary to remind people of the story of Abraham and Ishmael. Just as the pagans kissed the black stone, Mohammed kissed the black stone, and Muslims today believe that when they kiss the black stone it is pleasing to Allah.

MOHAMMED CHANGES THE QIBLAH

When Mohammed first began to receive his revelations, he instructed his followers to pray facing Jerusalem as the Jews did. During the early days of Mohammed's ministry, he still hoped that the Jews would accept his revelations and honor him as a true prophet. The Jews never accepted Mohammed as a true prophet. As Mohammed gained more followers and power, he turned strongly against the Jews who had rejected him. He believed that his revelations were far superior to any revelations the Jews might have.

One day during the noon prayer in Medina, Mohammed received a revelation from Allah telling him to use the Kaaba as the new Qiblah, the new direction of prayer. He was told that the old Qiblah was just a test, and now Allah gave Mohammed a more pleasing Qiblah. Instead of praying towards Jerusalem like the Jews did, Muslims should face the Kaaba.

> O Muhammad, many a time We noticed you turning your face towards heaven; now **We will make you turn towards a Qiblah that will please you.** Turn your face during Salah towards the Sacred Mosque (Kaaba); wherever you are turn your face in that direction. The people of the Book know this to be the truth from their Rabb. Allah is not unaware of what they do (Quran 2:144, F. Malik).

In this way the old house of idols became the center of Islamic worship. Mohammed received the revelation that the holy God, the creator of the universe, wanted everyone to bow down five times a day in the direction of a house of idols. The same place that was the center of worship for Arab idol worshipers became the center of worship for all Muslims.

BOWING DOWN TO THE BIG IDOL

Moses stated: "You shall not make for yourself a carved image—any likeness of anything that is in heaven above, or that is in the earth beneath, or that is in the water under the earth; you shall not bow down to them nor serve them. For I, the LORD your God, am a jealous God, visiting the iniquity of the fathers upon the children to the third and fourth generations of those who hate Me, but showing mercy to thousands, to those who love Me and keep My commandments" (Exodus 20:4-6).

Mohammed destroyed the 360 idols that were positioned around the Kaaba. He kept the big idol, the Kaaba itself. He kept the house of idols. The Kaaba is made by human hands. It is not to be bowed down to. To do so is idol worship.

Mohammed destroyed the small idols, but he kept the most important idols. He kept the Kaaba and the black stone. The black stone was the most important idol found in the Kaaba. Mohammed kissed this stone and pointed to it as he marched around the Kaaba, just as his idol-worshiping ancestors had done. Mohammed bowed down and prayed towards the Kaaba and the black stone five times a day. Every day, millions of Muslims follow his example.

Muslims will argue that Jews also pray towards Jerusalem. The Bible instructs the Jews to pray in this direction (II Chronicles 6:34). So what is the difference? Muslims pray towards the Kaaba; Jews pray towards Jerusalem.

The difference is that the Jews were not following a pagan practice as they prayed towards Jerusalem. The temple of Solomon was not a pagan temple. It was a temple carefully built according to the instructions of God. When idols were introduced into the temple of Solomon, the temple was destroyed. God does not allow his temple to be polluted with idols or by pagan ceremonies.

In contrast, the Kaaba was a place filled with idolatry and idol worship. The rituals of the Kaaba were there before the days of Islam. The Arabs worshiped stones in those days, and they still kiss the black stone that is in the Kaaba. The rituals of the Kaaba were the rituals of paganism and idolatry.

Blood sacrifices always involve covenant. In the spirit realm, a covenant is being formed when men sacrifice animals in a ceremonial manner. Today Muslims are required to make animal sacrifices as part of their pilgrimage to the Kaaba in Mecca. What covenant is being formed as they do this? Are they truly giving themselves to God in this covenant, or is a covenant being formed with something else?

God is a jealous God. When Muslims bow down to the Kaaba, they are bowing down to an idol. When they kiss the black stone, they are kissing an idol. When they march around the Kaaba and kiss the black stone, they are participating in the rituals of idol worship. When they make blood sacrifices, they are not making a holy covenant with God because God no longer accepts the blood of animals from his worshipers. They are making a covenant with someone else.

These rituals did not come from God. These rituals are not pleasing to God. The man who participates in them is not obeying God. He is rebelling against God.

Vaughn Martin

22 Blasphemy

Moses declared: "You shall not take the name of the LORD your God in vain, for the LORD will not hold him guiltless who takes His name in vain" (Exodus 20:7).

What does it mean to take the Lord's name in vain? It can mean to curse or blaspheme God. It also means to use the Lord's name wrongly. For example, if I would commit adultery and then claim that the reason I committed adultery was because God told me to commit adultery, I would be guilty of taking the Lord's name in vain. I would be guilty of blasphemy.

Suppose I began to steal from everyone I did not like. When I was caught stealing, I would claim that God had told me to steal. I would claim that I was God's special messenger, and that He allowed me to steal, unlike other messengers. If I did this, I would surely be guilty of taking God's name in vain. I would be guilty of using His name wrongly. Instead of using his name in a way that brings him glory, I would be guilty of using his name to justify my own sin. I would be guilty of blasphemy.

What if I lied to my wife? What if I was caught sleeping with another woman, and my wife caught me? When she caught me, I would not want anyone to know that I was sleeping with someone who wasn't my wife. So I would tell my wife that I would never cheat on her again, if only she did not tell anyone about what I had done. Suppose my wife was so angry with my cheating, that she went and told her friends about what I had done. Would it be okay if I then went to live with my lover? Would it be okay if I told everyone that I was allowed to break my promises to my wife because God told me it was okay to do so?

What if I lusted after the wife of my adopted son? Would it be okay if I convinced my son that God actually wanted him to divorce his wife so that I could marry her? Would it be right if I married that woman after my adopted son divorced her? Would it be right if I told everybody that God was the one who wanted my son to divorce his wife so that I could marry her?

If I did any of these things, I would be terribly guilty. I would be guilty of using God's name in vain. I would be guilty of using God's name to justify my lust, my lies, my covetousness and my theft. I would be guilty of blasphemy.

When a man uses revelations from God to justify his sins, his sins do not become holy. The sins remain just as sinful as they were before. The man simply adds blasphemy on top of all his other sins.

What if my ancestors were idol worshipers? What if I told everybody that God told me that we should worship Him by using the pagan ceremonies of my ancestors? What if I told everyone that God told me that we should worship Him by kissing a special stone, and by marching around an old temple that was full of idols in times past? What if I told everyone that they should bow down in the direction of this old temple five times a day? Would I be innocent or guilty of blasphemy?

Mohammed broke the laws of God. He committed adultery. He ordered the slaughter of his neighbors. He took his neighbors' possessions, lands, wives and children. He taught his followers to participate in the idolatrous rituals of his tribe. When Mohammed broke the laws of God, he prophesied in the name of God and said that God was the one who wanted him to break these laws. As he did these things, Mohammed took God's name in vain. He used God's name to justify terrible deeds.

SINNING IN THE NAME OF GOD

Mohammed oversaw the massacre of the Jews of Qurayza. Mohammed carefully chose a man named Sa'd ibn Mu'adh to decide the fate of the Jews of Qurayza. When Sa'd ibn Mu'adh made this decision, he was already dying from a wound that he had received in battle. In great pain, he gave Mohammed the answer that Mohammed wanted. He said that all the Jews should be killed. And so nearly 800 Jews who had never raised arms against Mohammed were beheaded, and their wives were taken as sex slaves. Mohammed justified the decision to murder the Jews by praising Sa'd ibn Mu'adh with the words: "You have given a judgment similar to Allah's Judgment" (Bukhari 5:148).

This is blasphemy. This is using the name of God in vain. God did not order Sa'd ibn Mu'adh or the Muslims to murder all the Jews. Sa'd and Mohammed made this decision , and it was an evil decision.

This is why so many terrible things are done in the name of Islam. Mohammed's followers believe that the righteousness of God is revealed in Mohammed. Everything Mohammed did, said, and prophesied must be followed.

Many of his followers today believe that because Mohammed married a six-year-old girl, they can do the same. Mohammed slaughtered his neighbors and took their wives as sex slaves, and evil men use the example of Mohammed to justify the same deeds today.

This is why the soldiers of ISIS (Islamic State of Iraq) can rape young girls and claim that God blesses their rape. This is why the soldiers of ISIS murder everyone who does not agree with them. They are following the example of Mohammed to the detail. They are using the name of God to justify terrible crimes.

When the followers of Mohammed do these things, they take the name of the Lord in vain. They use the name of God to justify horrifying crimes. They use the name of God to justify rape, murder, lying and stealing. Mohammed used the name of God to justify his crimes, and some Muslims today follow his example.

There are many instances in Mohammed's life in which he used "revelation" to get what he wanted. Sometimes what he wanted was a minor thing. For example, Mohammed was annoyed with visitors who stayed too long in his home instead of going home. He received the revelation,

> O you who believe! Do not enter the houses of the Prophet unless permission is given to you for a meal, not waiting for its cooking being finished-- but when you are invited, enter, and when you have taken the food, then disperse-- not seeking to listen to talk; surely this gives the Prophet trouble, but he forbears from you, and Allah does not forbear from the truth (Quran 33:53).

Do you really think that before the world was created, God wrote a book in which he told Mohammed's visitors not to stay too long in Mohammed's house?

On many occasions, Mohammed wanted to do something evil, and the only thing that could justify the evil he wanted to do was a revelation from God. Perhaps he wanted steal the possessions of his neighbors, or take his adopted son's wife, or break a promise he had made to his wives. In every case, he received a revelation that supported him in doing the evil thing that he wanted to do.

As you read the following examples, do you really think that God is the one who spoke to Mohammed about these things? There are many evil spirits in this world. There are many evil spirits that encourage men to sin and to rebel against God. These spirits even pretend to be God so that they can deceive people. If a revelation encourages you to do something that is evil, does that revelation really come from God?

When Mohammed coveted his son's wife, causing his son to divorce her so that Mohammed could marry her, Mohammed justified his covetousness with the revelation that Allah was the one who was giving Zaynab to Mohammed. It is written in the Quran, "We gave her to you as a wife…."

Mohammed was not rebuked by Allah for marrying his son's wife. He was rebuked because he hid in his heart what Allah had revealed to him while Zaynab was still married to his adopted son. Mohammed received the revelation in his heart that Zaynab was to become his wife while she was still married to Zaid (Quran 33:37).

When Zaid brought Mohammed's request of marriage to his former wife Zaynab as she was praying, she said. "I do not do anything until I solicit the will of my Lord." She remained praying in the mosque. Luckily for Mohammed, a revelation was given almost immediately to him that Allah was giving Zaynab to him as his wife (Quran 33:37). Zaynab accepted this revelation as the answer to her prayer and married Mohammed.

Mohammed received the revelation that the reason he was supposed to marry Zaynab was so that all Muslims would know that they were free to marry the wives of their adopted sons. However, even after receiving this revelation, it still didn't seem right to some that Mohammed had married his adopted son's wife. Luckily for Mohammed, he soon received the revelation that adopted sons were not real sons in the sight of God (Quran 33:5).

When Mohammed broke the promise he made to his wives that he would stop sleeping with Mary the slave girl, Allah told him that he should not try to please his wives by not sleeping with Mary. Allah also told Mohammed that it was okay for him to dissolve his oaths, as long as he made expiation for them.

> O Prophet! why do you forbid (yourself) that which Allah has made lawful for you; you seek to please your wives; and Allah is Forgiving, Merciful. Allah indeed has sanctioned for you the expiation of your oaths and Allah is your Protector, and He is the Knowing the Wise (Quran 66:1-2).

When Mohammed's wives began to unite against him because he took a slave girl into Hafsa's bed, Mohammed received a revelation. The Quran says that if Mohammed's wives unite against him, Allah will be his ally. If Mohammed would choose to divorce his wives, Allah will support his decision and give him better wives (Quran 66:3-4).

When Mohammed sent his men on raids against the Meccan caravans, he received the revelation that certain things were given to him that were not given to other prophets. Other prophets were not allowed to steal, but Mohammed was given the right to take booty. "The booty has been made Halal (lawful) for me yet it was not lawful for anyone else before me" (Bukhari 1:331). "So enjoy what you took as booty; the spoils are lawful and good" (Quran 8:69).

When Mohammed moved to Medina, he and his followers lived among Jews who were more prosperous than themselves. Mohammed soon received the revelation that the whole earth belonged to Allah and his apostle, and therefore he could drive the Jews out of Medina and take everything they owned.

When Mohammed wanted to banish the Banu Nadir and take their possessions, he received the revelation that they were about to drop a stone on his head. This revelation was used to justify his attack on them.

When Mohammed took the lands and possessions of the Banu Nadir and drove them out of Medina, he received the revelation that it was Allah who was forcing them to leave (Quran 59:3).

When Mohammed besieged the Banu Nadir, he ordered the date palm trees to be chopped down. The Law of Moses forbids the destruction of food-bearing trees when a city is besieged. Mohammed received the revelation that destroying the trees was ok, because it was Allah's will for him to do so (Quran 59:5).

Mohammed took the lands, houses, weapons, and other remaining possessions of the Banu Nadir for himself instead of distributing the booty among his soldiers in the usual way. He received the revelation that he did not need to share these possessions with his soldiers, because not much fighting was involved in chasing the Banu Nadir out of Medina (Bukhari 4:153).

When Mohammed tired of his wife Sauda, and made an agreement with her that he would not divorce her so long as he no longer needed to sleep with her, his decision was supported by a revelation from Allah. Mohammed's agreement might seem selfish to man, but the revelation that supports it is in the Quran (Quran 4:128).

Mohammed did not like people mocking and criticizing him. On a number of occasions, he sent out assassins to kill poets who mocked him. Mohammed received the revelation that those who mocked or criticized him were mocking and criticizing Allah. They were guilty of disbelief, and the penalty for a Muslim who disbelieves is death (Quran 9:64-66).

When Mohammed's men had taken both male and female captives at the battle of Hanain, the men wanted to rape the women, but they were not sure it was lawful to so because the women's husbands were present. Mohammed received the revelation, "And all married women (are forbidden) unto you save those (captives) whom your right hands possess" (Quran 4:24). And so his men were freed to rape their married captives after a waiting period. The hadiths show that sometimes Mohammed and his men did not wait at all.

When Mohammed wanted to break a treaty, he received the revelation that he could break any covenant if he feared treachery from his covenant partner

(Quran 8:58). Mohammed was quick to accuse non-Muslims of treachery, so this revelation allowed Mohammed to break any covenant that he wanted to break.

Mohammed entered into the treaty of Hudaybiyyah with the Meccans. The treaty stated that any Meccan who joined Mohammed in Medina would be sent back to Mecca. Mohammed did not want to send back the women who came to him. Predictably, Mohammed received the revelation that he did not need to keep the terms of the treaty that he had made with the Meccans. He received the revelation that these women were free to join him. He received the revelation that their marriages with non-Muslims were not lawful, and that Muslims could therefore marry them (Quran 60:10).

Women came and offered themselves to Mohammed. Mohammed received the revelation that he was permitted to have any women for himself who came and "dedicated her soul to him."

Mohammed really liked women. He received the revelation that he would be given many women in heaven. He received the revelation that believing Muslim men would have 100 times the sexual strength and desire in heaven that they had on earth (Sunan al-Tirmidhi 2459).

Mohammed wanted to meet with his followers on Friday, because Friday was market day in Medina and all the Muslims came to town on that day. He received the revelation that God originally gave Friday to the Jews, but they argued about it, and so it was given to the Muslims (Bukhari 2:1, and 2:21). Mohammed did not keep the Sabbath, but he received a revelation about the terrible judgment that came upon Jews because they did not keep the Sabbath. He received the revelation that Sabbath-breakers are cursed. He received the revelation that God hates the Jews and turned them into apes because they broke the Sabbath (Quran 2:65-66).

Worst of all, when Mohammed wanted to please his Arab followers, he received the revelations that instructed them to participate in pagan, idolatrous ceremonies. Mohammed's Arab followers grew up worshiping idols. The central focus of idol worship in the pre-Islamic days was the Kaaba in Mecca. Mohammed received the revelation that his followers were supposed to bow down and pray in the direction of the Kaaba five times a day. In this way an old house of idols became the center of Islamic worship.

Every Muslim is supposed to go on a pilgrimage to Mecca and the Kaaba at least once in his lifetime. When they arrive there, they are supposed to circle the Kaaba just as their idol worshiping ancestors did and kiss the black stone just as their idol worshiping ancestors did. They are supposed to circle the two mountains, As-Safa and Al-Marwah, just as their idol worshiping ancestors did. They are supposed to offer animals as sacrifices just as their idol worshiping ancestors did.

Did the Kaaba become holy just because Mohammed claimed that Abraham built it? Of course not. The Kaaba is still the same house of idols that it was before the days of Islam. It is still the house of the most important idol of the Arabs, the black stone. The ceremonies that take place there today are just as idolatrous as the ceremonies that took place in times past, before the days of Islam.

GOD TAKING SIDES

Muslims believe that the Quran is God's eternal, holy word, written before Creation began. Do you really think that before the creation of the world, God wrote a holy book, and that in that book He blessed all the sinful things that Mohammed wanted to do? Or do you think that maybe Mohammed prophesied according to his own desires and claimed that God was the source of the prophecy?

The Lord spoke to Moses, "The prophet who presumes to speak a word in My name, which I have not commanded him to speak, or who speaks in the name of other gods, that prophet shall die" (Deuteronomy 18:20).

Under the Law of Moses, the prophet who spoke his own words and said that they came from God was condemned to death. It is a very dangerous thing to prophesy according to your own desires. On the day of Judgment, every word will be judged. The man who sinned and said that God told him to sin will be judged very terribly indeed. It would be better for that man had he never been born.

23 You Shall Have No other Gods

The first of the Ten Commandments found in the law of Moses is "I am the LORD your God, who brought you out of the land of Egypt, out of the house of bondage. You shall have no other gods before Me" (Exodus 20:2-3).

It would seem that in this area, Mohammed and Moses are in complete agreement. At the very center of Islam is the revelation that there is one God and that no person should ever be raised to the level of God. Muslims believe that this revelation was given through many prophets in history, but that the message became corrupted and lost. They believe that God sent Mohammed as the seal of the prophets, to bring this message to the whole earth.

DO CHRISTIANS WORSHIP ONE GOD?

In Islam, there is one sin that is considered greater than any other, the sin of shirk. Shirk is the ascribing of partners to God, raising up someone or

189

something that is not God to the level of God. Many Muslims believe that Christians are guilty of shirk because Christians believe that God takes three different forms, even as He remains one God.

The Christian and Jewish scriptures emphatically state that there is one God. When Jesus was asked about the most important commandment in the entire Bible, he quoted this one: "Hear, O Israel: The Lord our God, the Lord is one. Love the Lord your God with all your heart and with all your soul and with all your strength" (Deuteronomy 6:4-5).

There is one God, and all other gods are false. So why do Christians worship Jesus? Christians believe that there is more than one expression of God. There is one God, but He comes in more than one form.

For example, in the natural world there are different forms of water. There is water vapor, a gas. There is liquid water. And there is ice. Each of these three forms of water is made of the same substance, water. Each form has exactly the same chemical makeup as the others, two atoms of hydrogen and one atom of oxygen, H2O. Although they are made of the same substance, the form each one takes is very different from the other.

Christians believe that God comes in three forms: God the Father, God the Son, and God the Holy Spirit. They believe that each of these three forms is God.

Christians do not believe that God took a wife. They do not believe that God married Mary and had a son. They believe that God takes three different forms and yet remains one God.

Sadhu Sundar Singh was an Indian man who became a follower of Jesus. Sadhu Sundar Singh did not only read the words of Jesus that are written in the Injil. Sadhu Sundar had many visions and dreams in which Jesus met with him and spoke with him. He travelled through the land of India telling Hindus, Moslems, and Sikhs about his Lord. Many miracles took place as he prayed for sick people in the name of Jesus.

Sadhu had many encounters with Jesus. On one occasion, he asked Jesus to explain to him how there can be one God, and yet that one God takes different forms. Jesus answered him, "Just as in the sun there are both heat and light, but the light is not heat and the heat is not light, but both are one, though in their manifestation they have different forms, so I and the Holy Spirit, proceeding from the Father, bring light and heat to the world. Yet We are not three but one, just as the sun is but one.

Neither of these descriptions fully explains the Christian view of the triune nature of God. God is simply greater than our ability to describe Him. God created the dimensions of time and space and is not bound by these dimensions. As humans, we are not able to fully understand how God can be one God and yet three persons. And yet this is the way that the scriptures describe Him.

It is true that Christians worship Jesus as God. Christians believe that Jesus is not a man who becomes God. Christians believe that in Jesus, God became man. They believe that Jesus came forth from God, and therefore He is called the Son of God. He is also called God the Son.

LIFTING UP MOHAMMED

In the Quran, shirk is repeatedly condemned. The man who received this revelation that no one should ever share the glory of God was Mohammed. Mohammed believed that Christians and Jews were guilty of this sin.

Muslims believe that Christians are guilty of this sin. Are Muslims innocent of this sin? Mohammed himself is raised very high in Islam. Muslims believe that Mohammed is the seal of the prophets. His word is lifted higher than all other prophets, even Jesus. Muslims believe that all other religious books are corrupted and that only the book that came through Mohammed is completely pure.

Muslims claim that Mohammed is not worshipped. However, if you look at the actions and deeds of Muslims, it is difficult to believe that Mohammed is not exalted to a level that is much too high. The Quran and the hadith clearly explain the many sins of Mohammed. In spite of this, Muslims treat Mohammed as if he is a perfect man, as if his example should be followed in everything. Muslims believe that the man who criticizes Mohammed in any way is an unbeliever. They base this extreme teaching on Quran 9:64-66.

Mohammed is a sinner. He set an example of lying, murder, adultery, stealing, and covetousness. He broke the Sabbath. He did terrible things in the name of God.

The Quran itself confirms that Mohammed is a sinner. This is not the testimony of Mohammed's enemies. This is the testimony of Mohammed himself. It is the testimony of both the Quran and the hadiths of Mohammed. In Quran 47:19, Allah commands Mohammed to repent of his sin, saying "Know therefore, that there is no god but Allah, and ask forgiveness for thy fault (sin) and for the men and women for believe."

Mohammed repented of his sins many times a day. He is recorded as saying "By Allah! I ask for forgiveness from Allah and turn to Him in repentance more than 70 times a day" (Bukhari 8:319). Mohammed prayed in this way "O Allah! Set me apart from my sins as the East and West are set apart from each other and clean me from sins as a white garment is cleaned of dirt (after thorough washing). O Allah! Wash off my sins with water, snow and hail" (Bukhari 1:711).

If you believe the Quran, then isn't it necessary to believe that Mohammed was a sinner?

THE PARTNER OF GOD

Mohammed is lifted very, very high by Muslims. He is lifted higher than any other prophet.

What does it mean to be a "partner" of God, to commit the sin of shirk? It means to share the worship of God. If a man receives the praise that should be given to God, he is guilty of shirk. Jesus said, "How can you believe, who receive the honor that comes from man, and you do not seek the honor that comes from God" (John 5:44)? If a man receives the praise that should be given to God, he is guilty of shirk.

In Islam, the sinner Mohammed is lifted very, very high. Muslims demonstrated with their actions just how much they idolized Mohammed. They struggled to catch the spit that came out of his mouth so that they could rub that spit on themselves. They fought over the water that he washed himself with. They even refused to look directly at him. The following hadith shows that Mohammed was more honored than any king on the earth:

By Allah, whenever Allah's Apostle spat, the spittle would fall in the hand of one of them (i.e. the Prophet's companions) **who would rub it on his face and skin**; if he ordered them they would carry his orders immediately; if he performed ablution, they would struggle to take the remaining water; and when they spoke to him, they would lower their voices and would not look at his face constantly out of respect. Urwa returned to his people and said, "O people! By Allah, I have been to the kings and to Caesar, Khosrau and An-Najashi, yet I have never seen any of them respected by his courtiers as much as Muhammad is respected by his companions. By Allah, if he spat, the spittle would fall in the hand of one of them (i.e. the Prophet's companions) who would rub it on his face and skin; if he ordered them, they would carry out his order immediately; if he performed ablution, they would struggle to take the remaining water; and when they spoke, they would lower their voices and would not look at his face constantly out of respect" (Bukhari 3:891).

Even worse, in the Quran and the hadith, there is no clear separation between the word of Allah and the word of Mohammed. Whatever Mohammed wants, Allah supports. When Mohammed speaks, it is assumed that everything that comes out of his mouth is the word of Allah. This is why there is such confusion in Islam.

Every true prophet needs to know the difference between his own words and the words of God. If he confuses these two things, he becomes a false prophet. Prophets are just people with the evil desires and sins that every person has. They are given the word of God. They must be very careful not to speak their own desires and claim that God is the one speaking through them.

As stated, in Islam there is no clear distinction between the words of Mohammed and the words of Allah. Likewise, there is no clear distinction between the decisions of Allah and the decisions of Mohammed. Whatever Mohammed decided to do was said to be supported by Allah. Nobody was ever allowed to challenge or test Mohammed to ask him, "Is your decision in this matter really from God?" The person who questioned Mohammed's decisions put himself in a very dangerous position indeed. Consider the following revelation that Mohammed received:

"It is not fitting a believer, man or woman, when a matter has been decided by Allah and his Apostle, to have any option about their decision. If anyone disobeys Allah and his Apostle, he is indeed on a clearly wrong path." (Quran 33:36)

This scripture makes it clear. When Mohammed speaks, God speaks. When Mohammed decides something, God has also decided something. No man is permitted to question that decision. Mohammed is the partner of God, and all his decisions, and all his words carry the authority of God.

What is shirk? It is receiving the praise that belongs to God. It is assuming that the decisions of a man are always the same as the decisions of God. It is believing that the words of a man are always the words of God. If any man in history has committed this sin, Mohammed has committed this sin.

Jesus is not a man who is exalted as a partner of God. Jesus is a manifestation of the Father, sent to earth to reveal God's love, salvation, and holiness to the world. In Jesus, God became man. In Mohammed, a sinful man is exalted as a partner of God. His words are never separated from God's words. His desires are always equated with God's desires.

24 The Qualifications of the Prophets

THE AUTHORITY OF ISLAM

In the end, what is the evidence that validates Mohammed's ministry? Why should men follow him? Mohammed broke the Law of Moses and the teachings of Jesus many times. Each time it happened, Mohammed justified his actions with a revelation. Muslims believe that the revelations received by Mohammed carry greater weight and authority than any other prophetic revelation received by any other prophet, and, therefore, Mohammed's actions are justified.

Muslims believe that there is no need for Mohammed's actions to be justified in any other way. Muslims believe that Mohammed didn't need to perform miracles, because the Quran itself is a miracle. They believe that the Quran itself is proof that Mohammed is the prophet of Allah.

THE SIGNS OF MOSES

When God sent Moses to deliver the children of Israel from Egypt, he didn't send Moses empty-handed. God gave Moses a staff that turned into a snake. When Moses spoke to Pharaoh, God released terrible plagues upon the Egyptians. As Moses led the Israelites out of Egypt, many miracles took place. The Israelites crossed over the Red Sea on dry land, while the Egyptian army was destroyed behind them. Bread came from heaven every morning to feed the people. Water gushed from the rocks at the command of Moses. The Israelites learned that their God was a God of miracles, a God whose power was far greater than all the false gods of the Egyptians.

The Israelites learned that if they walked closely with God, no evil power was able to harm them. When the enemies of Israel hired a powerful sorcerer named Balaam to try to place a curse upon Israel, Balaam was completely unable to curse Israel. Instead of cursing Israel, he blessed Israel. Balaam prophesied, "How shall I curse whom God has not cursed? And how shall I denounce whom the Lord has not denounced?" (Numbers 23:8).

"For there is no sorcery against Jacob, Nor any divination against Israel. It now must be said of Jacob and of Israel, 'Oh, what God has done!'" (Numbers 23:23).

Who can curse what God has blessed? Although the enemies of Israel sacrificed their own children to the devil to gain evil spiritual power, that evil spiritual power could not harm Moses or the Israelites when they obeyed God. God's power is so much greater than Satan's that there is no sorcery, no curse, and no witchcraft that can have any effect upon the true children of God.

On one occasion, as the children of Israel wandered through the desert, they came to a place known as Marah. By the time they arrived in Marah, they had run out of water, and had become desperately thirsty. In Marah there was water, but the water was extremely bitter and completely undrinkable. Moses cried out to the Lord for help, and the Lord showed Moses a tree. Moses cast the wood of that tree into the waters of Marah, and the water became sweet, and the children of Israel were able to satisfy their thirst.

At Marah, the Lord spoke to Moses, saying, "If you diligently heed the voice of the LORD your God and do what is right in His sight, give ear to His commandments and keep all His statutes, I will put none of the diseases on you which I have brought on the Egyptians. For I am the LORD who heals you" (Exodus 15: 22-27).

God gave great miracles and signs to his servant Moses, whom he protected from all the power of Pharaoh. The promises and protection of God were not only for Moses. The promises and protections of God were also for the children of Israel who obeyed the commandments of God.

The children of Israel were completely protected from the curses of sorcerers. At Marah the Lord promised to protect the Israelites from sickness and disease if they obeyed the Lord's commands. At Marah the Lord demonstrated that even poisonous, bitter water would be made sweet for His servants.

When Jesus came to this earth, he performed more miracles than any man in history. He raised the dead and gave sight to the blind. Every kind of sickness and disease was healed by Jesus. Jesus had authority over death and disease. He had authority over all the power of the evil one. The devil was completely unable to harm Jesus, until the day that Jesus gave his life as a perfect sacrifice to pay the price for sin.

This great authority of Jesus is also given to his followers. Jesus said to his disciples, "Behold, I give you the authority to trample on serpents and scorpions, and over all the power of the enemy, and nothing shall by any means hurt you" (Luke 10:19).

After Jesus rose from the dead, he spoke to the ones who followed him and believed in him: "Go into all the world and preach the gospel to every creature. He who believes and is baptized will be saved; but he who does not believe will be condemned.

"And these signs will follow those who believe: In My name they will cast out demons; they will speak with new tongues; they will take up serpents; and if they drink anything deadly, it will by no means hurt them; they will lay hands on the sick, and they will recover (Mark 16:15-18)."

Jesus gave his followers complete authority over the power of the devil. Witchcraft and curses cannot harm a true follower of Jesus. The man who believes in Jesus has a covenant with the living God, and he never needs to fear the power of the evil one. All over the world, witches and sorcerers know that their curses and sorcery have no effect at all upon true believers in Jesus.

Jesus gave his followers authority over sickness. The same authority that Jesus demonstrated over sickness is given to his followers. All over the world, true believers in Jesus lay their hands upon the sick, and the sick recover. This was true 2,000 years ago, and it is true today.

Jesus even gave his followers authority over poison, saying, "…if they drink anything deadly, it will by no means hurt them." He told them that even the poison of serpents would be unable to harm them. Even if they ate or drank poison, that poison would not harm them.

The servants of God are protected from the curses of the devil, from sickness and disease, and from poison. This protection is evidence that these servants belong to the living God and that He takes care of them. This protection is evidence that even when these servants of God are placed in the grave, the grave will not be able to hold them because they belong to God. On Judgment Day, they will be raised from the dead to live with the Lord forever.

THE SIGNS OF MOHAMMED

Mohammed never claimed to be able to perform miracles. There are many verses in the Quran that speak of the fact that God did not give supernatural signs (miracles) to Mohammed to prove that the Quran was sent from God. Muslims believe that it was not necessary for Mohammed to perform miracles because the Quran itself is a miracle. Consider the following verses from the Quran:

> Yet when the truth came to them from Ourselves, they said, 'Why has he not been given the like of that Moses was given?' But they, did they not disbelieve also in what Moses was given aforetime? They said, 'A pair of sorceries mutually supporting each other.' They said, 'We disbelieve both' (Quran 28:48).

> They also say, 'Why has no sign (ayatun) been sent down upon him from his Lord?' Say: 'Surely God is able to send down a sign (ayatan), but most of them know not' (Quran 6:37).

> They have sworn by God the most earnest oaths if a sign (ayatun) comes to them they will believe in it. Say: 'Signs (al-ayatu) are only with

God.' What will make you realize that, when it comes, they will not believe (Quran 6:109) ?

They say, 'Why has a sign (ayatun) not been sent down upon him from his Lord?' Say: 'The Unseen belongs only to God. Then watch and wait; I shall be with you watching and waiting' (Quran 10:20).

The unbelievers say, 'Why has a sign (ayatun) not been sent down upon him from his Lord?' Thou art only a warner, and a guide to every people (Quran 13:7).

Then, it may be that you will give up part of what is revealed to you and your breast will become straightened by it because they say: Why has not a treasure been sent down upon him or an angel come with him? You are ONLY a warner; and Allah is custodian over all things (Quran 11:12, Shakir).

Not before this didst thou recite any Book, or inscribe it with thy right hand, for then those who follow falsehood would have doubted. Nay; rather it is signs, clear signs (ayatun bayyinatun) in the breasts of those who have been given knowledge; and none denies Our signs but the evildoers. They say, 'Why have signs (ayatun) not been sent down upon him from his Lord?' Say: 'The signs (al-ayatu) are only with God, and I am only a plain warner.' What, is it not sufficient for them that We have sent down upon thee the Book that is recited to them? Surely in that is a mercy, and a reminder to a people who believe (Quran 29:48-51).

In this passage, we see that the "signs" that Mohammed brought were not miracles. The signs brought by Mohammed were the verses of the Quran. These verses are clear signs "in the breasts of those who have been given knowledge." The convincing arguments found in these verses are "clear signs" that the Quran comes from God. These convincing verses are sufficient for Muslims to believe, they do not need other miracles in order to believe.

Most Muslim scholars agree that Mohammed was not empowered to perform miracles. The Quran refers to Mohammed as a "plain warner." The only miracle of Mohammed is the Quran itself. Muslims believe that the Quran is a book that is clearly divine in its origin.

Mohammed's lack of authority over sickness and disease is also clearly seen in the hadiths. Jesus healed every form of sickness and disease, and even raised the dead. Mohammed did not have this authority. Therefore, Mohammed's teachings on sickness were very different from the teachings of Jesus. Instead of healing the sick and empowering his followers to heal the sick, Mohammed taught his followers that if they suffered in sickness, some of their sins would be forgiven.

> Narrated Abu Sa'id Al-Khudri and Abu Huraira: The Prophet said, "No fatigue, nor disease, nor sorrow, nor sadness, nor hurt, nor distress befalls a Muslim, even if it were the prick he receives from a thorn, but that Allah expiates some of his sins for that" (Bukhari 7:545).

> Narrated 'Abdullah: I visited Allah's Apostle while he was suffering from a high fever. I said, "O Allah's Apostle! You have a high fever." He said, "Yes, I have as much fever as two men of you." I said, "Is it because you will have a double reward?" He said, "Yes, it is so. No Muslim is afflicted with any harm, even if it were the prick of a thorn, but that Allah expiates his sins because of that, as a tree sheds its leaves" (Bukhari 7:551, 550).

When Mohammed suffered under sickness, he claimed that his suffering would bring him a double reward from Allah. In other words, Mohammed believed that sickness was actually a kind of blessing from Allah, because when one suffered from sickness his sins would be forgiven and he would receive a reward. Mohammed said, "If Allah wants to do good to somebody, He afflicts him with trials" (Bukhari 7:548).

Mohammed suffered very much from sickness. Mohammed's wife Aisha said, "I never saw anybody suffering so much from sickness as Allah's Apostle" (Bukhari 7:549).

WITCHCRAFT AND MOHAMMED

Mohammed not only suffered from disease, he also suffered under the influence of witchcraft. The hadiths testify of the time when Mohammed was bewitched. Black magic was used against the prophet so that he began to think he was doing something that he was not actually doing. Mohammed became so severely confused that he thought he was doing one thing, while in fact he was doing another. He thought he was sleeping with his wives, while in fact he was not.

The hadiths testify that this magic was carried out by Lubaid bin Al-A'sam. This man had obtained some of Mohammed's hair from a comb and used that hair to place a curse upon Mohammed. This hair was combined with some pollen from a date palm and placed in a well. After suffering under this black magic for an entire year, Mohammed prayed and received revelation in a dream about the witchcraft that had been used against him.

> Narrated'Aisha: The Prophet continued for such-and-such period imagining that he has slept (had sexual relations) with his wives, and in fact he did not. One day he said, to me, "O 'Aisha! Allah has instructed me regarding a matter about which I had asked Him. There came to me two men, one of them sat near my feet and the other near my head. The one near my feet, asked the one near my head (pointing at me), 'What is wrong with this man? The latter replied, 'He is under the effect of magic.' The first one asked, 'Who had worked magic on him?' The other replied, 'Lubaid bin Asam.' The first one asked, 'What material (did he use)?' The other replied, 'The skin of the pollen of a male date tree with a comb and the hair stuck to it, kept under a stone in the well of Dharwan.'" Then the Prophet went to that well and said, "This is the same well which was shown to me in the dream. The tops of its date-palm trees look like the heads of the devils, and its water looks like the Henna infusion." Then the Prophet ordered that those things be taken out. I said, "O Allah's Apostle! Won't you disclose (the magic object)?" The Prophet said, "Allah has cured me and I hate to circulate the evil among the people." 'Aisha added, "(The magician) Lubaid bin Asam was a man from Bani Zuraiq, an ally of the Jews" (Bukhari 8:89, also see 7:660).

Witchcraft and sorcery never come from God. Witchcraft and sorcery are the works of jinn, devils, witches and sorcerers. People pay sorcerers money to use the powers of evil spirits to curse their enemies.

Jesus and his followers were completely protected from these evil powers. Evil spirits feared Jesus more than anything in this world. Jesus cast out evil spirits with a single word, and his followers were given authority to do the same. Mohammed was not protected from the power of these spirits, and neither are his followers. This is not the testimony of the enemies of Islam. This is the testimony of the most respected hadiths in Islam.

MOHAMMED AND POISON

Not only was Mohammed unprotected from disease and sorcery. He was also completely unprotected from poison. In fact, it was poison that killed Mohammed.

After the battle of Khaybar, a Jewish woman offered Mohammed a meal of roasted sheep. The Muslims had just killed the woman's father, uncle, and husband. In spite of this, they didn't think it was suspicious when she offered them this feast.

In fact, the woman had poisoned the sheep. As the men began eating it, one Muslim named Bishr immediately fell dead. Mohammed said, "Lift your hands (from eating), for it has informed me that it is poisoned!" Mohammed sent for the woman to ask her why she had poisoned the sheep. The woman answered, "If you were a prophet, it would not harm you; but if you were a king, I would rid the people of you." Mohammed ordered the woman to be executed (Abu Dawud 4498).

Mohammed's death from poisoning did not take place immediately. Mohammed did not eat enough of the poisoned sheep to die immediately. For two years, the poison worked in his body, slowly killing him. After two years, he was in such a miserable condition that two men needed to carry him around with his arms draped over their shoulders as his feet dangled uselessly (Bukhari 3:761).

Many have speculated about the cause of Mohammed's sickness. Mohammed himself was not in doubt. He knew that he was suffering from the poisoned sheep that he ate at Khaybar. As he suffered, he said to his wife, "O Aisha! I still feel the pain caused by the food I ate at Khaybar, and at this time, I feel as if my aorta is being cut from that poison" (Bukhari 5:713).

Aisha said of her husband, "I never saw anyone suffer more pain than the Messenger of Allah" (Sunan Ibn Majah 1622).

And so Mohammed died of poisoning. It might seem to be a humiliating death for a prophet to be killed by a woman. Mohammed had prayed many times that he might die in battle. Instead, Mohammed was poisoned by a Jewish woman.

In fact, Mohammed's death was not only painful and humiliating. Mohammed's death was much worse than that. It is written in the Quran:

And if he had invented false sayings concerning Us, We assuredly had taken him by the right hand and then **severed his life-artery (aorta)** (Quran 69:44-46 Pickthal).

According to the Quran, if Mohammed was a false prophet who invented words from Allah, Allah would kill Mohammed by cutting his life-artery, his aorta. Mohammed himself testified when he was dying from poison, "O Aisha! I still feel the pain caused by the food I ate at Khaybar, and at this time, I feel as if my aorta is being cut from that poison" (Bukhari 5:713).

The Quran states that if Mohammed was a false prophet, God would kill him by cutting his aorta. As he was dying, Mohammed himself testified that he felt his aorta being cut by the poison. If you believe the Quran, this is evidence that Mohammed's death was actually caused by God.

Mohammed spoke many terrible things in Allah's name. When he desired another man's wife, he declared that Allah was giving him that wife. When he wanted to lie, he claimed that Allah was the one allowing him to lie. When he wanted to steal, he claimed that Allah gave him permission to take booty. We have listed many of these examples in this book.

At the end of Mohammed's life, why did God not rescue Mohammed? It is such an easy thing for God to heal a man. Jesus walked in complete authority over every kind of sickness, as did his followers. If Mohammed was such a beloved prophet of God, why did God not heal him? Why did he allow Mohammed to die such a painful, humiliating death? Is it possible, that Mohammed's death was a kind of judgment from God? Is it possible that Mohammed spoke wrongly in the name of God many times, and that at the end of his life God judged him for his many false prophecies?

The only thing that can possibly be used to justify the deeds of Mohammed are the revelations of Mohammed. Mohammed performed no miracles, and he broke the law of Moses and the teachings of Jesus many times. However, Mohammed received revelations from Allah that told him that he was supposed to do these things.

But even the revelations of Mohammed found in the Quran testify that Mohammed was a false prophet. Mohammed received the revelation that if he spoke wrongly in the name of Allah, Allah would kill him by cutting his aorta. How did Mohammed die? By his own testimony, his aorta was cut by the poison he received at Khaybar. If even the Quran itself testifies that Mohammed was a false prophet, then what is left? Is there any evidence that Mohammed was sent from God, or received revelations from God?

Why do so many people believe that Mohammed will lead them to Paradise? Mohammed was a sinner. This is the testimony of the Quran, which repeatedly speaks of the need for Mohammed to repent of his sins. It is the testimony of the hadiths and the Sirat, which list Mohammed's sins in great detail. In spite of all this evidence, people believe that the revelations of Mohammed are reliable and will show them the way to Paradise.

Mohammed does not know the way to Paradise. Mohammed cannot save himself, and he can certainly not save anyone else. Near the end of his life, Mohammed testified: "Say (O Muhammad): 'I am not a new thing among the Messengers (of Allah) (i.e. I am not the first Messenger) nor do I know what will be done with me or with you. I only follow that which is revealed to me, and I am but a plain warner'" (Quran 46:9).

In this verse, Mohammed declares that he does not know what will be done with him. He declares that he is just a "plain warner." Mohammed does not know if he will enter Paradise or not. Mohammed does not know what will happen to him on the Day of Judgment.

25 The Perfect Sacrifice

This book is written to help the reader find the narrow road that leads to life. There is a broad road that leads to destruction, and most people are walking on that road. There is a narrow road that leads to life, and only a few find it.

All have sinned and fallen short of God's righteousness and glory. The price of sin is death. God is holy, and the sin of people must be paid for. There is a perfect sacrifice that pays the price of a person's sin and makes it possible for that person to come to God and enter Paradise.

On the Day of Judgment, Mohammed will not be able to save himself, and he will not be able to save anyone else from the judgment of God. Likewise, on the Day of Judgment, Moses will be unable to save himself or anyone else. Moses was a sinner just like Mohammed.

Moses wrote down the Law that God gave him, but Moses did not completely keep the Law. Moses murdered an Egyptian. Moses was almost killed by God after he argued with God and had not circumcised his sons. Moses disobeyed God and struck the rock twice that brought forth water instead of speaking to it. For these sins and others, Moses was forbidden to enter the land that God promised him. Moses was a sinner and a law-breaker. He died as all sinners do and was buried in the ground.

Moses received the Law of God, but that law will not save him. That law will condemn him. The Law of Moses exposes the sin of every man and condemns every man.

The Law of Moses shows every man that he is a sinner. If we study the life of Mohammed using the Law of Moses, we discover that Mohammed is a sinner who broke the laws of God. If we look carefully at any man's life using the Law of Moses, we will discover that the man is a sinner. Which man has not lusted after a woman? Which man has not lied? Which man has always honored his parents? Which man has been perfect as God is perfect?

Now we know that whatever the law says, it says to those who are under the law, that every mouth may be stopped, and all the world may become guilty before God (Romans 3:19).

Why would God give a law to mankind, that no one can keep? Why would He give us a law that demands that we be perfect as God is perfect? Who is as perfect as God?

Everyone has sinned, and the price of sin is death. Who can pay the price of sin? What hope is there for any living person?

The Law is given so that every person would know that he needs a perfect sacrifice. God has made a way that a person can come to him. God has made a sacrifice that breaks the power of sin in a person's life. With this sacrifice, a person's sins can be forgiven and removed.

In the Bible stories, we see a shadow of this perfect sacrifice. When God sent his angel to visit the homes of the Egyptians and the Israelites in Egypt, the Israelites were instructed to take the blood of a perfect lamb and to put that blood on their doorposts. When the angel visited the homes of the Israelites, he saw the blood of the lamb that was on the doorposts of those homes. And so the angel "passed over" those homes, and did not harm the sinners who lived there. However, when the angel of the Lord visited the homes of the Egyptians, every home that did not have the blood of a perfect lamb on its doorpost suffered the loss of its firstborn son.

When God comes in judgment, there must be a perfect sacrifice to pay the price of each person's sin, so that he will not be destroyed by God. The blood of the perfect lamb that was placed on the doorposts of the Israelites was a prophecy that pointed to the perfect sacrifice that would come.

Jesus is the perfect sacrifice. Jesus is the perfect Lamb of God. When John the Baptist saw Jesus, he had a revelation. He prophesied, "Behold the Lamb of God, who takes away the sin of the world!" Suddenly, John understood who the real Lamb of God was.

Jesus is the sacrifice that not only covers sin. He is the sacrifice who destroys the power of sin. When a person believes in Jesus, the blood of Jesus cleanses him from all sin. His sins are completely forgiven.

Jesus is the Passover Lamb. Just as the blood of the lamb saved each family from death, it is the blood of Jesus that saves mankind from destruction. He takes away the sin of the world.

When Mary was pregnant with Jesus, an angel came to her husband Joseph and said that his wife would "bring forth a son, and you shall call His name Jesus, for He will save his people from their sins" (Matthew 1:21).

Jesus is the Passover Lamb. He is the Savior of mankind, the One who saves people from their sins. If you repent of your sins and believe in Him, your sins will be forgiven. He paid the price for your sins on the cross.

Of all the deceptions that came through Mohammed, the greatest deception is found in the claim that Jesus never died on the cross. If Jesus did not die, then we have no hope. If Jesus did not die, then every man must pay the price for his own sins. The price of sin is death. Every man must die and enter hellfire if his sin is not paid for. But God in His great mercy gave us a Lamb that would give his life for us. Just as the Passover Lamb died so that each family of Israelites could be saved, Jesus died so that our sins could be paid for, and we can be rescued from death and hell.

GOD WITH US

In the Injil, Jesus is called Emmanuel, which means "God with us."

Why was it necessary for God to come to earth as a man? God the Father is holy and pure, dwelling in unapproachable light. We cannot come to this holy God. Our sins have a penalty attached to them, the penalty of death. If we come into the presence of such a holy God, we will immediately die.

And yet God deeply loves us, every man and woman He has created, and wants us to come to Him. God knows that we are all lawbreakers. He knew that no matter how much we tried to keep His law, we would fail. He knew the sin and lust that was in our heart. He knew that we could not pay the price of our sins. And so He decided to pay the price for us.

We could not come to Him because of our sin, but He came to us. God took on human flesh and came to earth as a man, the Son of God calling himself the son of man. God himself became the perfect sacrifice that pays the price for our sin. Because the price has been paid, we can become the people of God, connected to Him in covenant.

THE CROSS

Two thousand years ago, Jesus entered Jerusalem on the 10th of Nisan, the day when the Jews were selecting perfect lambs for their Passover feast. When Jesus entered Jerusalem riding on a donkey, people celebrated his arrival. They laid palm branches on the ground, and declared that he was the chosen one, the Masih. The city received its perfect Lamb, the Lamb of God on the same day that every family was choosing its Passover lamb, to be slain for the Passover feast.

On the 14th of Nissan, the Jews celebrated the Passover feast, in memory of the day they were saved from death by the blood of the Lamb. On the 14th of Nisan in Jerusalem Jesus gave his life for his people. He was murdered by the Jews and the Romans on a cross. He died just like a Passover lamb dies, to pay the price of sin for his people so that they might live.

On the day that Jesus went to the cross, he was betrayed, and put on trial by evil men. At his trial, even his accusers could find no sin in him.

In spite of his innocence, the people demanded his death. The religious Jews hated Jesus because He exposed their sinfulness. The Roman soldiers hated Jesus because He represented a kingdom much greater than the Romans. Finally, the authorities gave way to pressure from the crowd that hated Jesus, and they agreed to have Jesus executed. Jesus was tortured and hung on the cross to die by evil men.

The one man who had conquered sin, was tortured to death on a cross. This seems like a terrible defeat for a prophet. In fact, it was not a defeat. Just as Jesus conquered sin, he also needed to conquer death. He needed to give his life as a sacrifice, to pay the price for the sins of all who believed in him, to pay the price for the sins of all his followers.

Many Muslims think that God would never allow one of his prophets to be tortured to death in the way that Jesus was. They believe that Jesus never died on the cross, that he only appeared to die.

In fact, it is true that nobody could force Jesus to die. Jesus was far more powerful than all the devils, jinn, and evil men. Jesus could have spoken a word and ten thousand angels would have immediately rescued him. Jesus had no sin, so he did not need to die.

Jesus chose to die. When the crucifixion was approaching, Jesus spoke of his coming trial. He talked of the relationship with his Father, a relationship so close that he would even give his life if it were the Father's will. He said, "Therefore, my Father loves me, because I lay down my life, that I may take it again. No one takes if from me, but I lay it down of myself. I have power to lay it down, and power to take it again. This command I received from my Father" (John 10:18).

Jesus chose to give his life. Nobody could take it from him, because he was without sin. So why did He die? Jesus died because he was the Lamb of God. He died for you, and he died for me. He died so that our sins could be paid for, so that we can be reconciled to God.

When Jesus died, he died sinless as the perfect Lamb of God. He gave his life as a gift to all those who would follow him. As he died, he paid the price for sin. However, because he had never committed sin, he was actually paying the price for the sins of his followers, the sins of those who believe in him.

And on the 17th of Nissan, three days later, the city of Jerusalem celebrated the feast of first fruits. On that same day, women came to the tomb of Jesus and found that it was empty. He had risen from the dead. The Bible says that Jesus is the first fruits of those who believe. Many will be raised from the dead and will enter Paradise, but Jesus was the first. He is the first fruits of the harvest of those who are raised from the dead to enter Paradise.

THE BLOOD COVENANT

When you believe in Jesus, you enter a blood covenant with him. The blood of Jesus was shed on the cross, and the man who believes in him enters a blood covenant with him. Believers in Jesus take part in a covenant ceremony, in which they remember the blood covenant that they have formed with Jesus.

The night before Jesus went to the cross to die, he led his disciples in this ceremony. He took a piece of bread, gave thanks for it, broke it and gave it to his disciples. He said to them, "This is my body which is given for you; do this in remembrance of me."

Then he took a cup of wine, and gave it to his disciples, and said to them, "This cup is the new covenant in my blood, given for you; do this in remembrance of me."

In this way Jesus declared to his disciples that he was about to give his blood for them, so that they could enter into a blood covenant with him (Luke 22:19-20).

In a blood covenant, two become one. In the blood covenant of marriage, a man and a woman share everything, including their possessions and their bodies. In the blood covenant that a person forms with God, a person gives everything he/she has to God, and God gives everything He has to the person.

The only thing a person has that does not come from God is his sins. Everything else he has, every possession, and even his own body, was given to him from God. When a person enters a blood covenant with God, God takes his sin. The sin is given to the Lamb of God, who carries that sin on his shoulders. The Lamb of God takes that sin and pays the price for it, so that a man can live. The Lamb of God paid the price for sin when He died on the cross.

In this blood covenant, God takes our sin upon Himself and pays the price of sin. In this covenant, everything that God has is made available to us. Because Jesus rose from the dead, those who enter into covenant with him will also rise from the dead and live with him forever.

THE RESURRECTION

Jesus died for mankind's sin and paid the price for that sin. He was put in the tomb for three days. After three days in the grave, Jesus rose from the dead.

This is not just a story. This resurrection is a proven fact. Jesus appeared to his disciples after his resurrection. He also appeared to many others. All in all, he appeared to about 500 people after his resurrection.

Jesus appeared to Mary Magdalene, who was one of his followers. Mary was weeping at the tomb of Jesus, because she believed that he was dead. Jesus appeared to Mary and said to her, "Do not cling to me, for I have not yet ascended to my Father; but go to my brethren and say to them, 'I am ascending to my Father and your Father, and to my God and your God'" (John 20:17).

This is an amazing scripture. In a blood covenant, two become one. When people believe in Jesus, they enter into a covenant with him. They enter into a covenant with the living God. This covenant is why Jesus told Mary to send the message to his disciples, "I am ascending to my Father and your Father, to my God, and your God.'" Just as Jesus has a relationship with his Father, his followers who are in covenant with him can also have a relationship with the Father. They become the children of the living God.

The victory of Jesus becomes the victory of his followers because of the blood covenant that is formed through the blood of Jesus Christ. Jesus triumphed over death. Death could not hold him in the grave. Jesus defeated death. He rose from the dead and appeared to many. Then he ascended into heaven, where he is seated at the right hand of the Father. Those who believe Jesus also receive this victory. The grave will not hold them. On the Day of Resurrection, they will arise to live forever.

Jesus knew where he came from, and where he was going. He said to his followers, "Even if I testify on my own behalf, my testimony is valid, for I know where I came from and where I am going" (John 8:14).

Jesus said to his followers, "Let not your heart be troubled; you believe in God, believe also in me. In My Father's house are many mansions; if it were not so, I would have told you. I go to prepare a place for you. And if I go and prepare a place for you, I will come again and receive you to myself; that where I am, there you may be also. And where I go you know, and the way you know" (John 14:1-4).

THE JUDGE

Jesus said, "For the Father judges no one, but has committed all judgment to the Son, that all should honor the Son just as they honor the Father. He who does not honor the Son does not honor the Father who sent Him" (John 5:22-23).

The Injil reveals that judgment has been committed to the Son. Jesus is not only the perfect lamb, the perfect sacrifice, who paid the price for our sins. Jesus is also the perfect judge.

Who is qualified to judge man's sin? Who is qualified to judge any man, or condemn any man? Is a sinner able to judge sinners?

Judgment has been given to Jesus because he is the only one who has actually kept the laws of God. He is the only one who truly demonstrated the righteousness of God. The Son walked as a man, and was tempted as a man, and yet did not sin. The Son is God, but he took on human flesh and walked as a man, with all the same weaknesses, and temptations that a man faces.

Jesus walked in complete unity with his father. The Bible says that out of the heart, the mouth speaks. In the same way, when we say that Jesus was sinless, we are saying that his heart was in complete unity with the Father. Everything he said, and everything he did came from the heart of the Father. He loved people with the love of the Father. He blessed people with the blessing of the Father. There was no difference between his heart and words, and the words of the Father.

This is why Jesus said to his followers, "I and My Father are one" (John 10:30). Jesus and his Father walked in such unity that it was impossible to completely separate them. He came forth from the Father, and He revealed the Father to the world.

Jesus said, "He who has seen me has seen the Father" (John 14:9).

THE PERFECT JUDGE IS THE PERFECT LAMB

This perfect judge is also the perfect lamb. The same one who is appointed to judge you has died for you, to pay the price for your sin. If a man is guilty, deserving of death, and standing before a judge, who can rescue that man? Can a judge really order another man to pay the price of the first man's sin? He cannot.

But what if the judge himself decides to pay the price for that man's sin? What if the judge declares the man's guilt and decides to pay the penalty himself? What if the judge himself accepts the death penalty that the sinner deserves?

This is what Jesus has done for us. The love of God is difficult to comprehend because our love is so limited. Man has rebelled against God in a thousand ways, and yet God has made a way for man to return to God.

When you stand before the judgment seat of Christ, every sin and every word will be exposed by the one who loves you, the one who died for you. If you are a believer in Christ, your sins will be forgiven when you stand there. Sin and iniquity will be completely removed from your life, and you will enter Paradise. The place of judgment will become for you the place of grace and salvation.

THE LIVING CHRIST

Would you like to know that your sins have been completely forgiven? Would you like to know in your heart that you belong to God and that He will never let death or hell hold you? Would you like to be a child of God? Those who have a covenant with God will also be raised from the dead to live with God forever. They will not remain in the grave. They will not be cast into hellfire. They will follow the Lamb of God into heaven. They will become the sons of God because their sins will be completely removed.

Many Muslims are meeting Jesus. Many Muslims have become tired of religious rituals. Even though they pray five times a day and go to the mosque, they are not convinced in their heart that they will enter Paradise. They desire to follow God, but they don't know how.

Many Muslims know that by following the example of Mohammed, they are not coming closer to God. They know that even if they follow Mohammed's example to the smallest detail, they are not coming closer to Paradise. They know in their hearts that their sins are not forgiven.

If you want to be certain that your sins have been forgiven, you must come to Jesus. When you do, He will speak to your heart and you will know that He has taken away your sins. You will know that you are loved by God, and that He has not condemned you.

Jesus is alive. This is not a theory; this is a fact. Today, many people are meeting Jesus. Jesus is not just a theory, or a doctrine, or a philosophy. Jesus is alive. He answers those who call upon His name and brings them into a relationship with God.

This is the open door that is before you. It is not an easy door to enter. It is a difficult door, and a narrow path that only a few find. If you go through this door, many will hate you and reject you. They will accuse you of many things. But in your heart, you will know that you have found the way to Paradise.

People are proud. A person does not like to admit the need of a savior. A person does not like to admit the need for someone to pay the price for his sins. A person likes to think that he is good, and that he can enter Paradise because he is good.

The Law of Moses demonstrates that people are not good, that every person has sinned. The person who desires to enter Paradise must humble himself and confess that he needs a savior, that he cannot save himself. The person who desires to enter Paradise must repent of his sins and call upon the name of Jesus. He will receive an answer.

The proud person will not do this. The proud person will always judge others. He will always think that he is righteous and godly, even though he has broken the laws of God. The humble person will cry out to God and will call upon the perfect sacrifice that can remove his sin.

Every person needs Jesus. Jesus is not just for the Jews, or the Christians, or the Americans. Every Somali who hopes to enter Paradise needs Jesus. He needs the perfect sacrifice that will completely pay the price for his sin. He needs the help of the one who overcame death, the one who rose from the dead, if he hopes to enter Paradise when he dies. Likewise, every Arab needs Jesus. Every Arab needs the perfect sacrifice to pay the price for his sin.

CHANGED BY THE SPIRIT OF GOD

The man who follows Jesus will be changed by Jesus. Jesus died on the cross so that our sins may be forgiven, and so that we can enter a blood covenant with the living God. When you enter this covenant, not only will your sins be forgiven. You will also be changed.

The same One who has the power to forgive sins also has the power to change hearts. When a person turns to Jesus, repenting of his sin and putting his trust in Jesus, he enters a covenant with the living God. Because of this covenant, the Spirit of God enters that person's heart. The Spirit of God begins to work in that person's life. If that person obeys the Spirit of God, his heart will change. He will begin to love others with the love of God. He will begin to look like Jesus.

This is the power of the gospel of Jesus. Because of the covenant, the Holy Spirit of God is able to dwell in the hearts of people. The Holy Spirit of God changes a person's heart. The Holy Spirit removes the lust, bitterness, and hatred that lives in a person's heart. The Holy Spirit fills a person's heart with good things. In this way, a person begins to walk in the righteous ways of God.

When the Spirit of God comes upon a person who believes in Jesus, this Spirit also brings the power of God. The Holy Spirit of God gives gifts to the followers of Jesus, gifts of power. Those who believe in Jesus may receive gifts of healing, gifts of prophecy, or gifts of miracles. Because of the covenant, the same power that Jesus walked in is made available to His followers.

CONCLUSION

There is only One who fulfilled the Law. There is only One who demonstrated the righteousness of God. There is only One who can save us from our sins.

If you follow Mohammed, you are following a lawbreaker, and you will surely die in your sins. If you believe in Jesus and follow Him, your sins will be forgiven, and He will make a way for you to enter heaven.

All the true prophets testified of Jesus. The Torah and the Injil testify of Jesus. Jesus fulfilled the Law of Moses. He did not sin. He performed many miracles, healing the sick and raising the dead. He gave his life as a perfect sacrifice, so that the price of a person's sin could be paid. Because He was sinless, the grave could not hold Him. He rose from the dead and ascended into heaven, where He is seated at the right hand of the Father. He is coming soon.

ABOUT THE AUTHOR

Vaughn Martin is a man who loves God and seeks the scriptures to learn more about Him. If you would like to have personal contact with Vaughn, you can reach him at **vaughnmartin7@gmail.com.**

Made in the USA
Middletown, DE
14 October 2023